Supporting Early Speech-Language Development

Learn how to support developmentally rich language learning environments during a child's first eight years of life! This book demonstrates how to build foundations for a strong communication system, distinguish typical and disordered speech and language, and develop a deep understanding of the brain and language development connection. Featuring clear guidance on how to work with parents and speech-language pathologists, educators will find easy to implement strategies for supporting healthy communication and navigating any stumbling blocks in the early childhood classroom.

Kimberly A. Boynton is a certified speech-language pathologist with licenses in the areas of Speech Language Pathology, Director of Exceptional Services, and School Superintendent. She is currently Assistant Professor in the Department of Speech Language Pathology at Saint Mary's College in Notre Dame, Indiana.

Other Eye On Education Books
Available from Routledge (www.routledge.com/k-12)

Early Literacy Matters: A Leader's Guide to Systematic Change
Carol E. Canady and Robert Lynn Canady

Coding as a Playground: Programming and Computational Thinking in the Early Childhood Classroom, Second Edition
Marina Umaschi Bers

Culturally Responsive Self-Care Practices for Early Childhood Educators
Julie Nicholson, Priya Shimpi Driscoll, Julie Kurtz, Doménica Márquez, and LaWanda Wesley

Implementing Project Based Learning in Early Childhood: Overcoming Misconceptions and Reaching Success
Sara Lev, Amanda Clark, and Erin Starkey

Advocacy for Early Childhood Educators: Speaking Up for Your Students, Your Colleagues, and Yourself
Colleen Schmit

Grit, Resilience, and Motivation in Early Childhood: Practical Takeaways for Teachers
Lisa B. Fiore

Supporting Early Speech-Language Development

Strategies for Ages 0–8

Kimberly A. Boynton

NEW YORK AND LONDON

First published 2021
by Routledge
52 Vanderbilt Avenue, New York, NY 10017

and by Routledge
2 Park Square, Milton Park, Abingdon, Oxon, OX14 4RN

Routledge is an imprint of the Taylor & Francis Group, an informa business

© 2021 Kimberly A. Boynton

The right of Kimberly A. Boynton to be identified as author of this work has been asserted by her in accordance with sections 77 and 78 of the Copyright, Designs and Patents Act 1988.

All rights reserved. No part of this book may be reprinted or reproduced or utilized in any form or by any electronic, mechanical, or other means, now known or hereafter invented, including photocopying and recording, or in any information storage or retrieval system, without permission in writing from the publishers.

Trademark notice: Product or corporate names may be trademarks or registered trademarks, and are used only for identification and explanation without intent to infringe.

Library of Congress Cataloging-in-Publication Data
A catalog record for this title has been requested

ISBN: 978-0-367-54181-1 (hbk)
ISBN: 978-0-367-54065-4 (pbk)
ISBN: 978-1-003-08810-3 (ebk)

Typeset in Palatino
by SPi Global, India

To my niece and nephew, Isabelle Marie and Carter Julius, who have afforded me the opportunity to share my love of speech, language, and literacy learning with them. Sharing in your language learning journey brings immeasurable joy to my speech-language pathologist heart. The endless giggles, warm hugs, joyful laughter, and endless communication of your "great ideas," creative thoughts, heartfelt feelings, and beautiful insights will be some of my most cherished life memories. Being your Aunt Kim is one of my greatest gifts.

Contents

Meet the Author viii

Acknowledgements x

1 Introduction 1

2 Play and the Ages and Stages of Speech and
  Language Development 18

3 Brain Development and Language 47

4 Vocabulary Building and Phonological Awareness:
  The How and Why 63

5 Building the Optimal Communication Environment
  for all Communicators 81

6 Children with Speech and Language
  Delays or Disorders 100

7 The Communication Breakdown 117

Meet the Author

Kimberly A. Boynton, Ph.D., CCC-SLP
Dr. Kimberly Boynton is a licensed and certified speech-language pathologist holding the ASHA Certificate of Clinical Competence, Indiana Professional Licensing Agency Speech-Language Pathologist license, Indiana Department of Education licensing in the areas of Speech-Language Pathology, Director of Exceptional Services, and School Superintendent. She has speech-language pathology experience working with children ages birth to high school in various practice settings, including early childhood education settings, public and private schools, home-based services, and private practice settings. She received a Bachelor of Science degree in Audiological and Speech Sciences and a Master of Science degree in Speech Language Pathology from Purdue University. She received her Director of Exceptional Learner's License in 2013 from Ball State University. In 2019, she received her Doctor of Philosophy degree in Educational Administration from Indiana State University. Dr. Boynton has held clinical and administrative positions in the field of education. She has focused her work in the area of high-quality early childhood services, including significant work on community-level committees and task force groups to support and empower children and families. School-based experience has focused on the provision of speech and language assessment and intervention services, educator professional development, teacher evaluation system implementation, grant writing and management, and development and implementation of early childhood services. Dr. Boynton worked as a Director of Early Childhood Services within a large urban public-school district in Northern Indiana, working collaboratively with community early childhood programs and Head Start. Additionally, she studied and led the implementation of early childhood programming in a

large urban public-school district to support the community's need for additional early childhood opportunities for children and families. She has held the position of Coordinator of Early Childhood/Preschool Special Education ensuring equitable and appropriate services for all children. Additionally, she is a member of the Reach Out to Connect Kids (ROCK) community team in Elkhart, Indiana, offering collaboration with conversations about the connection between communication and behavior, as well as supporting continued advocacy for all children to have the strategies and tools necessary to support effective communication during the early childhood years through supporting classroom educators, children, and families. Current work as an Assistant Professor in the Department of Speech Language Pathology at Saint Mary's College in Notre Dame, Indiana, provides the opportunity to teach, serve, and conduct research in the area of Speech-Language Pathology, specifically school-based assessment and service delivery in the areas of speech sound and language delays and disorders. She currently teaches undergraduate and graduate speech-language pathology courses in the areas of childhood speech and language development, assessment, and intervention, and provides clinical supervision to graduate student clinicians.

Acknowledgements

I want to acknowledge my valued mentor and dear friend, Kay Tompkins. She was the coordinator of the early childhood education program where I began my career as a young and excited speech-language pathologist. She encouraged and supported my love of the collaborative opportunities within the early childhood and speech-language pathology fields. She empowered me to professionally grow and develop my clinical skills, working in partnership with parents, educators, and early childhood colleagues, sparking an ongoing enthusiasm for the positive impact that we can make for young children and families. Over the years, she has provided a sounding board for organizing my thoughts and problem-solving ways to better support children and families, supportive words when I was faced with new challenges that ultimately resulted in personal and professional growth, and enthusiastic encouragement when I pursued new career and professional growth adventures. Her knowledge, guidance, and supportive insight have been a pillar of my professional and personal growth and I am forever thankful for her mentoring and friendship.

Thank you to everyone at Routledge Taylor & Francis Group, including the editors, copyeditors, and all who shared in the work, including Misha and Olivia, who patiently answered all my questions and helped make this book a reality with their ongoing guidance, insight, and meaningful feedback.

I want to thank all of the children and families that have invited me into their lives, to work in partnership with them, in order to support speech and language acquisition, development, and use. I have learned more than I can convey in words from these children and families. My appreciation for these opportunities for partnership continues to grow exponentially. To all of the wonderful children and families – you inspire me to continue supporting the acquisition, development, and use of effective, functional communication. I look forward to my continued learning and growing with children and their families in the future.

I am also forever grateful to all of the talented and committed early childhood educators and colleagues I have worked alongside, as we planted communication seeds and built supportive bridges for effective communication. The work you do each day is so valuable and important for young children. I have learned so many lessons from you and the wonderful collaborative discussions we have shared.

With each new step on my personal and professional journey, I must acknowledge the need to recognize and honor the commitment of my parents, George Weil and the late Mary Weil, who sparked my love of learning. When I reflect back to my early childhood years and the memories I recall, I distinctly recall many wonderful books, visits to the library, being read to each day, and play-based interactions and learning, which I am certain supported the love of language learning that grew over my early years and continues in my life today.

Finally, but most importantly, a heartfelt thank you to my husband, Chris, my best friend and greatest support – I am truly thankful for your ongoing, steadfast patience, heartfelt support of my personal and professional growth, and for your partnership as we walk together on this life journey.

1

Introduction

The concept of this book grew out of many years of my speech-language pathology clinical practice in a variety of settings, including early childhood education and intervention, PreK-12 school experiences, private practice, and now teaching and clinical supervision in higher education. The realization of this book from my continued desire to serve as a collaborative partner with talented, committed, and caring parents and early childhood educators. Regardless of the setting of my clinical practice, teaching, and learning, my focus on supporting positive and effective communication for all individuals, with a particular commitment to young communicators, remains my steadfast goal. I convey the importance of this work to the students I teach in my college classrooms in each course I teach. I encourage these aspiring, future speech-language pathologists to reflect on effective communication and communication breakdowns with enthusiastic critical thinking and reflective problem-solving. When I am actively engaged in clinical practice opportunities, I reflect on and continue to make note of the various scenarios and associated interactions supported by effective communication. It is the reason I continue to strive to learn and grow in my understanding of speech and language assessment and intervention, as well as the theory and brain development associated with our communicative function, processes, and interactions. I have been inspired over the years by the young children and families I have been invited to work with, as well as the knowledgeable colleagues and aspiring student clinicians who work collaboratively to build strong supports for young communicators within the natural settings of their daily lives.

My various clinical experiences, spanning from birth through high school, have been solidly based in evidence-based, speech-language pathology practice serving children and families during their early childhood years and beyond, combined with my desire to provide a collaborative and practical presentation of speech and language information for early childhood educators. My passion for supporting young children and families during the early childhood years has continued to grow during my career as I have continued to find consistent evidence of the importance and value of developing a strong foundation for speech and language development beginning during the earliest years, through positive and authentic speech and language learning opportunities. Early childhood educators, caregivers, and parents are central and essential participants in the process of the acquisition and development of a young communicator's speech and language learning journey. Providing robust, language-rich environments, combined with various opportunities for children to actively engage in meaningful communication exchanges as participants, not observers, builds a means for ongoing growth and development for future effective communication use.

I continue to be afforded so many wonderful and exciting experiences and opportunities in my clinical practice to participate in the planting of language and speech learning seeds that support the encouragement and growth of a continuous love of learning with our youngest learners. Additionally, I find ongoing joy in the opportunity to work collaboratively with families and early childhood educators to support the building of communication bridges to support effective and functional communication during the development and use of speech and language in the early childhood years, across multiple natural environments in the daily life context of young children. My practical experience, joined with my literature review, as well as clinical knowledge I have developed during my years of clinical practice, in the areas of early childhood education theory and practice, speech acquisition and development, and language development and use, offer a platform for sharing thoughtful and practical ideas to utilize in a young child's natural environment to support the complex and dynamic role of communicating thoughts, ideas, needs, and emotions, as well as, following directions, understanding routines, and answering questions. These strategies, tools, and ideas are not meant to be exhaustive in nature, but instead offer considerations, springboards for additional ideas, and affirmations to support the valuable and robust speech and language development activities already embedded into many early childhood educators' classrooms and young children's home environments. Our youngest learners and their families offer us the opportunity to join them on their learning journey through engaging in supportive activities and strategies to encourage their creativity, join in their imaginative excitement, and travel on the journey with them as they acquire and develop important speech and language skills needed for the ongoing growth of effective, efficient, and functional communication.

When the communication system works effectively and efficiently, we generally find joy in our interactions and often seek out additional opportunities to connect with others. I strive continuously to find ways to support this joy and success of communication for all young children, regardless of their current communication skills and modes. Consider the idea that all children are communicating with us, but the means of communication will vary dependent upon the situation, as well as the skills and communication modes in the child's communication profile. My hope in writing this book is that it will provide practical, easy to implement ideas you will want to consider implementing. Additionally, I hope you will find new and fun strategies to try, or perhaps the desire to revisit some previous strategies you haven't used recently with the young learners engaging in communication exchanges in your life. The journey of speech and language acquisition and development is an exciting and ongoing path with several twists and turns, some barriers and roadblocks, and sometimes a need for planting seeds for continued growth or building of bridges to support stronger, more effective communication. The seeds we plant for future communication growth and the bridges we build with young children, to encourage the sharing of ideas in the early years, are important to this ongoing speech and language acquisition and development. Additionally, the ongoing effective use of the skills acquired in natural settings is a central focus for generalizing the skills into a child's routines, daily activities, and communication with peers and adults. Keep in mind the important consideration that the foundation you help build is extremely important as a child transitions into early elementary school, the upper elementary years, middle school, high school, and then post-secondary life. When we pause to consider the impact of the strong foundation built during the early childhood years, we begin to realize the reality that we only see a glimpse of the child's use of these skills, but we often have the distinct honor of seeing the potential of children's bright and exciting futures as they grow in confidence and independence to chart their own unique learning and life path. The speech, language, and literacy foundation during these early childhood education years, specifically during the critical birth to eight years, contributes to reading, writing, and overall literacy development in years to come. As early childhood educators, the positive impact you make in the lives of young children is realized for years after they leave your classroom, as they take the next step in their education and life journey with the communication skills, persistence, and excitement for learning instilled by parents and educators during their early years of life.

It will benefit us to introduce the concept and importance of literacy in our daily lives and interactions. The foundation will support our ongoing discussion in the chapters found within this book. I think we likely have all observed that we live in a literate society with reading and writing at the core of many opportunities and interactions. Consider the ways we obtain and process information in our lives, during our routines, within our work and educational settings, in our homes, and within social situations. Academic and social literacy are equally influential in the lives of all individuals, including reading books, social media, restaurant menus, signs, and other information methods and platforms. Understanding and utilizing the appropriate use of speech and language in interpersonal interactions, as well as understanding and use of academic or more formal language in formal education or work settings, both serve a role in effectively engaging in and navigating the world around us. In my opinion, it is impossible to minimize the role that literacy plays in our personal, educational, and societal lives. Understanding the impact that early naturalistic play-based learning opportunities have in the building of speech and language skills may have an undeniably important link to considering the role of literacy across contexts, listeners, and various daily situations as children learn and grow. The early childhood years provide excellent opportunities to teach, practice, and support future complex communication through building a strong, stable, and generalizable foundation, built upon play-based, developmentally appropriate, naturalistic learning and growth opportunities.

As a speech-language pathologist, I embrace the joy and reward of effective communication, but I also often frequently observe, firsthand, the frustration and disappointment of communication breakdowns in homes and classrooms, on playgrounds, and in a variety of other natural contexts and environments in a child's life. The breakdowns can occur between a variety of communication partners, including adults or children, and in a variety of situations. Additionally, these communication breakdowns may occur for a variety of reasons. The causes of communication breakdowns may be obvious or may require more analysis of the situation to determine the reason for the ineffective exchange, resulting in a communication breakdown. Regardless of the reason for the breakdown in effective communication, the ineffective result of communication attempts often causes frustration, reluctance to continue attempting communication, or reduced communication confidence, particularly with recurring failed attempts. A single communication breakdown may cause frustration, but recurring breakdowns may result in reluctance to attempt or engage in future communication exchanges. I find myself considering this impact with each individual child I work with to determine how to approach building bridges for immediate short-term and continued long-term communication success.

There is no way to deny that communication is an essential part of our daily lives, including nonverbal and verbal means. We use communication to engage in and navigate the world around us. Unsuccessful attempts to engage in expressing oneself or understanding the meaning of vocabulary, answering questions, or following directions may inhibit a child's learning and may also result in challenging social interactions. When we consider the many opportunities, we have each day to communicate, including language expression and comprehension, we also must consider the possibility of various communication breakdowns impacting overall effective and functional communication attempts that can also occur. We communicate in various ways each day through words, signs, gestures, pictures, and facial expressions. Additionally, we hear, process, understand, and respond to various receptive communication stimuli in our natural environments that provide important information for the navigation of the world around us. Effectively engaging in communication within our various environments requires the systematic combination of expressing ourselves and understanding communication input. The combined verbal and non-verbal system of communication is built on social rules, language expression, language understanding, and the use of the language modalities. It isn't enough for us to understand the domains and modalities of language. We must then be able to incorporate and use them effectively in the context of our daily lives. In some cases, the use of these language skills in the context of daily life is where the breakdown occurs. Perhaps a child understands the structure and system of language or sounds, but is unable to effectively use these skills across natural contexts in daily communication encounters. These various and often complex modes of communication are simply a glimpse at the multiple and varied verbal and nonverbal ways we communicate, as well as process and respond to auditory stimuli in a variety of situations and environments. Many of us utilize language each day without a thought about the complexity or speed of our communication processing and exchanges. We may give little thought or consideration to what we communicate verbally, as well as the associated non-verbal communication. In fact, these communication exchanges may occur automatically with high levels of effectiveness as a result of our solid and generalizable communication system. The complexity of communication may not be a consideration in our daily interactions due to our ability to utilize the communication system with little to no breakdown. Perhaps, you haven't ever paused to think about how you knew someone was upset, happy, or frustrated without explicitly using words to state her feelings. Have you considered the impact of nonverbal communication when your friend, who was talking on the phone, pointed to the paper on his desk you were there to pick up, to indicate you have permission to take the paper without him pausing from his phone conversation? How did you process, understand, and respond to the message he was delivering without the explicit use of verbal communication? Perhaps we only pause to consider the complexity of these systematic language interactions when a breakdown occurs. This is reasonable and expected, given that analyzing and problem-solving isn't necessary during each communication interaction, but it may be worth pausing briefly to identify that communication is a complex system regardless of the need to reflect and critically think on a daily basis about our communication encounters.

I would encourage you to pause for a moment and consider all the ways you communicate each day. Consider how many times you communicate on a daily basis. I am guessing too many to count and recall. I am a speech-language pathologist, so I admittedly communicate a great deal each day. In fact, like many of you, too many times to accurately quantify daily into numbers of attempts and interactions without setting up a specific systematic method of data collection for that purpose. I would venture to guess many of us communicate more than we realize through our verbal and non-verbal interactions. Do you use gestures, words, facial expressions? Do you find yourself utilizing one of these more than others in your communication exchanges? Are there ways you convey you are happy, sad, or mad without words? Have there been instances when someone knows how you are feeling or what you are thinking before you speak a single verbal word? When observing others engaging in communication exchanges, do you notice messages conveyed without words? What does the calm teacher with a warm smile greeting a child at the classroom door convey? How about the young child in the block area who is pointing and jumping up and down with excitement sharing his success at building a tall tower that hasn't fallen over yet? Or the mother with a big smile and tears streaming down her cheeks as her young child refers to her as "mama" for the first time? These are only a few examples of verbal and nonverbal communication exchanges that could occur in our daily interactions. These communication exchanges hold significant meaning without verbal expression. There are too many examples to describe and count. They are often individualized to the communicator and the situation. Consider the connection between our nonverbal and verbal communication. Perhaps you have experienced scenarios when the verbal and nonverbal communication didn't appear connected. Additionally, we can find meaning in the context of a situation, making a known context helpful, and often times essential for an effective communication exchange. Context can offer breadth and depth of understanding and meaning to a communication exchange. In fact, I have observed the introduction of contextual information positively impact the effectiveness of a communication exchange on many occasions in my years of clinical practice. Consider the role contextual cues, background knowledge, or shared information about a particular topic has played in the effectiveness of communication exchanges you have engaged in during your daily interactions.

Communication is a platform spanning all languages, contexts, and scenarios connecting us with each other and the world around us. Communication provides speakers and listeners of all ages with opportunities to use verbal and nonverbal language to express, understand and respond, engage in reciprocal communication exchanges, and convey thoughts, feelings, and opinions. Adults and children alike have a desire to communicate effectively and efficiently in a variety of situations with a multitude of communication partners. I think many of us may agree that ineffective and inefficient communication exchanges do not leave us feeling satisfied and may result in feelings of frustration or may make us reluctant to attempt novel communication exchanges.

While communication appears simplistic and basic on the surface when we engage in our daily communication interactions; if we stop to think about the what, how, and why of communication, we begin to uncover nuances, complexities, and variations of effective and optimal communication.

As we move forward progressing through the chapters in this book with the exploration of communication, including the areas of speech and language, I will provide opportunities for *Communication Connections* at various points. These connections to communication experiences will provide an opportunity for your consideration, reflection, and critical thinking to take root. Please consider using these *connection opportunities* for individual or group discussion. These pauses in the book content will offer opportunities to explore various components and topics of communication and the associated interactions and encounters. I believe we can learn a great deal through reflective practices, both individually and collectively, that can shape new considerations, build opportunities for modifications, adaptations, or expansions of current practices, encourage the potential for continued professional and personal growth, and offer needed, deserved, and valuable affirmations for all the important work you do each day with young children, their families, and caregivers. Exploring aspects of our own personal communication, as well as communication with young children has the potential to develop more reflective thinking practices for analyzing effective communication and communication breakdowns experienced with our youngest communication learners. Let's pause and explore the first *Communication Connection* to begin thinking about the complexity of communication and the potential breakdowns that may occur during our various and complex communication attempts.

COMMUNICATION CONNECTION

Consider a time when you were unable to communicate effectively. How did you feel? Did you feel frustrated or possibly defeated by your attempt to communicate? How did you handle the situation? Did you persist with determination or did you choose to completely abandon the attempt to communicate your thoughts, opinions, or feelings; or your attempt to process and understand during the communication exchange? Consider the following questions related to your specific scenario to analyze the communication breakdown and associated factors. Below each question I have provided an explanation of why these questions may be important to consider when a communication breakdown occurs.

1. **Who were you communicating with?**
   It is important to realize that communicating in situations with a single communication partner compared to a group of communication partners, with various nonverbal and verbal communication occurring simultaneously, has the potential to shift the complexity of the situation. Often in a group situation, multiple people contribute to a conversation with varied nonverbal and verbal communication. This requires the ability to gain, maintain, and sustain attention with a potentially evolving topic with multiple contributing individuals. It requires a level of joint attention focused on the specific topic of discussion. Turn-taking, asking, and answering questions, knowledge of the topic vocabulary, background contextual information, and filtering out background distractions are all factors to consider that may increase the communication complexity when participating in a group conversation.

   Additionally, considering your communication partner(s) is an important factor. Communicating with a familiar compared to unfamiliar communication partner also has the potential to impact the communicative exchange. When we communicate with a known individual, we may be accustomed to their communication style and use of frequent nonverbal and verbal communication modes to convey meaning. This known knowledge and context can allow more language processing and expressive energy to be spent on the actual conveying and receiving of messages. It may also result in more willingness to persist when a communication breakdown occurs due to the increased comfort level with the individual communication partner. Take a moment to reflect on your communication exchange with an individual who you regularly communicate and interact with and compare these interactions to communication with a new individual. What factors impact these communication encounters? Have these factors impacted the effectiveness of your communication exchanges? Now, returning our attention to the focus of our *Communication Connection*, what were the details of your communication exchange partner(s) in the communication exchange you chose to analyze?

2. **What were you trying to communicate?**
Consider the familiarity of the topic, unknown or known context, background knowledge, and the related details. When you and your communication partner(s) share known and understood knowledge of the conversation topic, including vocabulary and contextual information, this often provides known factors that will support effective communication without explicitly communicating each detail related to the communication message. Communicating details about a known topic may decrease the barriers to effective communication; however, in situations with shared known context and terminology, explicitly communicating each detail is often not necessary. Revisit your identified scenario. Did you and your communication partner(s) share knowledge of the topic? If you shared knowledge of the topic, in what ways did this make communicating more efficient and effective? In alternative situations, in what ways did lack of shared knowledge of context, vocabulary, or background knowledge impede the communication process?

3. **How were you communicating?**
   We often think of communication in terms of words verbally spoken, but think about the gestures, body language, and other nonverbal communication included in each of our communication exchanges. Verbally spoken words are only one aspect of the communication experience and it is important to consider all components involved in the communication of a message. Can you think of a time when a person's verbal words did not match the tone of the communication or the body language of the person? Those situations have the potential to send mixed messages or result in confusion about the conveyed message. Have you ever experienced a communication exchange involving an unclear message due to confusing nonverbal and verbal messages that weren't aligned and consistent?

   Consider how you communicated in your chosen scenario. Did your verbal communication, body language, and tone align, or did they potentially contribute to the communication breakdown? Did your communication partner's reciprocal nonverbal and verbal communication offer clarity or confusion to the communication attempt?

4. **Why was there a communication breakdown?**
   This is a big picture question that often does not have a simple answer or a simple solution. Analyzing communication breakdowns, including reflective practice with the questions I have provided, combined with finding ways to build communication bridges to support more effective communication, is always my goal as a speech-language pathologist. My beginning steps generally involve identifying the root cause of the communication breakdown and then moving forward in a direction to build bridges for individuals experiencing communication breakdowns; however, my ultimate goal is to provide the skills and build the solid foundation necessary for individuals to independently build their own bridges, to effectively communicate

when breakdowns occur in future interactions. I would like to tell you this is an easy process and that I have all the answers for making all communication attempts immediately effective with a single strategy or communication tool. It would be wonderful if we all just needed to use one single effective communication strategy, but we all know there isn't a single answer for all situations. In some cases, it is easy to identify the root cause and, with some minor supports, we can build a strong bridge resulting in highly effective and rewarding reciprocal communication exchanges, empowering young communicators through building independence and confidence. In other cases, it is complex with a combination of factors contributing to the decrease of communication effectiveness. Building multiple bridges comprising the use of many and potentially changing strategies may be necessary. Additionally, even with strategies to support expressive and receptive language, some communication attempts will not result in the desired outcome of an effective communication attempt. This highlights for us, once again, the ongoing complexity and dynamic nature of the communication process.

5. **What was the result of the communication attempt?**
What was the final result of your communication attempt? Was it successful or did it result in an ineffective and perhaps frustrating communication exchange? Did it involve follow-up communication attempts or clarifications? Did you abandon the communication attempt? Were you able to understand and express messages effectively?

Taking time to reflect on a situation that is specific to your personal communication attempts and breakdowns offers an opportunity to understand the value of analyzing individual communication exchanges, in order to build stronger tools for effective communication. Understanding that we all experience situations involving effective communication, as well as less effective communication exchanges will guide us in identifying and analyzing the effective communication and communication breakdowns experienced by our young communicators. This will provide us necessary information to determine strategies, tools, and goals to support ongoing communication growth and development. Pausing to consider the complexity of a personal communication attempt and associated communication breakdown helps us to build a better understanding of the multiple factors in each communication exchange. As we can see from our reflection and analysis, communicating is not an easy task! It is complex with many variables, multiple language domains in play working simultaneously, that require coordination and use. When communication works, it brings us joy and fulfillment, but the same is not true when it breaks down. Communication breakdowns vary in complexity from the need for a simple repetition or clarifying statement to the inability to effectively communicate or understand a message resulting in a true ineffective communication attempt.

Now, let's, think about your young child or a young child in your classroom, who you may have observed experiencing a communication breakdown with you, a parent, another adult, a sibling, or another same-age peer. Let's consider a child who has ongoing, recurring challenges with expressive and receptive communication due to decreased accuracy of speech sound production, lack of vocabulary or background knowledge, difficulty understanding questions or following directions, or difficulty combining words into sentences to convey meaning. Imagine the potential frustration, sadness, lack of motivation, or possible decrease in confidence, that may result from ongoing communication breakdowns and challenges with the children we care for and educate each day. Have you ever watched a young child's frustration grow with recurring ineffective communication attempts? Perhaps, a less desirable behavior appears or the child retreats from novel or regular communication attempts? In fact, it may appear that a young child is reluctant to follow directions, when, in fact, the child is unable to understand and process directions of varying length and complexity. I have observed these communication breakdowns many times in my work as a speech-language pathologist. I would suspect that many of you have experienced the same observations in your home or classroom at times. I have watched young children conveying potential frustration, sadness, and anger by demonstrating inappropriate and undesirable actions or retreating and shutting down. I have engaged in many collaborative conversations with determined, committed educators and parents to analyze and find ways to support a young child in finding effective ways to express and understand language during acquisition, development, and use. This ongoing need to support young children with communication acquisition and development provides me with the strong drive and commitment to continue to advocate for optimal communication environments for all communicators because I value the importance of effective communication within our daily interactions. I know many educators, parents, and fellow speech-language pathologists walk along this optimal communication advocacy path with me and I am thankful to be part of such a robust and committed team. We need to consider that young children experiencing expressive, receptive, and/or social language deficits may feel ongoing frustration or communication fatigue daily within our classrooms. The fatigue can manifest as undesirable behaviors, including acting out, shutting down, withdrawing from social interactions with peers, or reluctance to answer questions or share ideas.

Parents and early childhood educators can work together as a team to build a positive communication environment for all children in our care. Your role as a valuable communication builder contributes to the planting of seeds for the growth of our youngest learners into confident, motivated, and functional communicators, regardless of their method and level of communication. As we plant the necessary seeds and build the supportive, solid bridges for positive communication opportunities, we are then afforded front row seats to watch children flourish, find happiness, engage in the world around them to learn and grow, and share their unique opinions, feelings, and ideas.

Early childhood, specifically the important birth to eight years old timeframe, is a critical time to begin building the foundation for a strong communication system. Your important role as an early childhood educator plays an integral part in building a solid language foundation for current and future communication, speech, language, and literacy learning. Ongoing collaboration with parents, caregivers, and early childhood education colleagues provides a springboard for a future of effective communication, including expressing, understanding, socially interacting, reading, and writing for all of our young learners. This important time in a young child's life provides opportunities for learning through experiences, modeling, play-based, and authentic interactions.

My hope is the following chapters in this book will provide an opportunity for you to explore and reflectively consider ideas for continuing to build and enhance language rich and language learning environments during a child's first eight years of life. I believe whole-heartedly in the important collaboration among and between parents, early childhood and early elementary educators, and additional early childhood development and education colleagues who provide learning and growth opportunities for children each day. I write this book combining my years of clinical practice with a literature review of theory, empirical evidence, and evidence-based speech-language pathology practice at the core, with a steadfast and sincere belief that we can support all children in achieving effective communication and building a strong foundation for future literacy learning.

As we begin to engage in the ongoing discussion of exploring the importance and impact of literacy learning, it is essential to remind ourselves that literacy is found everywhere in our daily lives. Supporting children in building a strong literacy foundation during the early childhood years provides needed skills for reaching their potential and the opportunity for meaningful engagement in the literate world. My experience as a speech-language pathologist has afforded me collaborative opportunities spanning various environments, professional disciplines, and families with diverse needs. Regardless of the setting, the collaborative nature of parents and early childhood educators, combined with the desire to build communication bridges and plant seeds for future and ongoing literacy and learning growth, reinforces the importance of the critical early childhood years.

In the following chapters, you will find a review of typical, delayed, and disordered speech and language acquisition and development, as well as the brain and language development connection. We will examine the potential adverse impact of trauma on a child's ability to effectively communicate within a variety of situations and environmental contexts. Additionally, we will discuss the importance of phonological awareness and vocabulary knowledge. We will explore strategies to support the generalization of skills across a young child's natural environments by focusing on building optimal communication environments for all of our young communicators, based on individual strengths and needs. My hope is you will find the following chapters to include easy to implement ideas for continuing to build an optimal and effective communication environment built upon enhancing your language rich classrooms. You will find ideas for navigating those inevitable communication breakdowns in the early childhood environment and opportunities for reflective practice to identify ways to enhance your language rich environment and scaffold opportunities to meet the needs of your individual and diverse young communicators, as they learn and develop speech and language skills. Although many of the concepts, theory, and strategy will be provided within a general context, I hope you will consider ways to utilize the information specific to the individualized needs of the young children in your life. *Communication always counts*, so let's begin our exploration of speech and language acquisition, development, and learning!

2

Play and the Ages and Stages of Speech and Language Development

As a speech-language pathologist, I am consciously and consistently aware that my work with early childhood educators, early elementary school educators, parents, and caregivers continues to push me to think about the acquisition, development, use, and impact of speech and language in a variety of ways within the natural contexts of a young child's life. I never tire of this area of study and the opportunities to learn additional and new knowledge to support young children and their families. In my opinion, we need to begin our conversation with the focus on naturalistic environments and contexts to achieve optimal effective communication results for young children. Natural context is an important consideration that we will revisit often in our exploration of speech and language development. Effective communication needs to happen in a child's natural settings, including home, school, the playground, at soccer practice, and in the lunchroom to name a few common early childhood contexts. Of course, as a speech-language pathologist, I am excited when a young child reaches mastery of a speech or language skill working with me in intervention settings outside the natural environment, but I know the most important aspect of my work is to ensure the child's communication skills generalize to the natural environments of his or her daily life. It won't benefit the child's effective and functional communication in a recognizable way if that generalization to natural contexts and across various scenarios doesn't occur.

Communication is a complex and dynamic system. It is often a fast-paced system of expression and comprehension, requiring a combination of verbal and nonverbal skills. In a communication exchange, there is a need for sustained attention, expression, comprehension, and social language. I can say with absolute confidence that I do not have all the answers for easily ensuring effective communication in every situation, but I have learned to approach every new communication challenge with a collaborative spirit, a need to support individual communication needs, and a strong commitment to critical thinking and problem-solving to support the building of solid and strong communication bridges for the youngest language learners. Approaching communication breakdowns with an information-gathering and problem-solving approach often leads to the reward of successful, effective communication. I find joy in the fact that I will always have the opportunity to continue learning and growing with my colleagues, the children I work with, and their families as we find ways to continue to plant communication seeds and build bridges for effective communication and ongoing learning. I find excitement in the opportunity to collaborate with parents, early childhood educators, and caregivers to identify the root cause of communication breakdowns and begin to build support for overall effective communication that will carry forward with a child in school and life across various situations and settings. Being part of a child's communication journey is an honor and I will continue to work to advocate for every child's right to engage in meaningful and fulfilling communication exchanges and opportunities in all environments. I hope you will see this journey as a way to empower the young learners in your classroom or the young child in your home to reach the level of effective communication that provides reward and satisfaction during interactions. In order to begin developing a plan for planting seeds and building bridges for effective communication, we need to first review or build an understanding of each area of communication and the accompanying speech and language domains, including developmental milestones and expected trajectories.

Areas of Communication

Communication is a broad term that encompasses many different components of speech and language necessary for a functional and effective communication experience. We must begin with the understanding that the overall goal is effective communication exchanges, which provide an avenue for oral and written expression, listening and reading comprehension, and meaningful social interaction. Doesn't that sound simple enough? Someone talks, someone listens, and perfect communication takes place, right? It is a simple and easy combination of speaking, writing, listening, and understanding, right? In some cases, it is, in fact, just that simple, but as we all know and as I mentioned in Chapter 1, at times, it becomes significantly more complicated. We have likely all observed challenges with this *effective communication process* play out; perhaps with our own communication exchanges or those encountered with the children you teach and care for each day or your own young communicator. Individuals, children, and adults, may experience frustration if they are unable to find the right words, convey their emotions, answer a question, formulate a sentence, follow a direction, or describe a situation. These are only a few of the many purposes of effective expressive and receptive communication. There are several components within a successful communication experience that we need to consider. Children may experience difficulties with one, several, or even all of these components resulting in a communication breakdown. The exciting news is that once we identify the aspects contributing to the communication breakdown, we can begin to build supportive bridges to strengthen overall functional communication in the young child's natural environments.

Who is the Speech-language Pathologist?

Before we dive into an in-depth exploration of the domains of speech and language specifically, I want to provide information about the role of the speech-language pathologist. Most people have a basic understanding of what speech-language pathologists do, but understanding all the roles and responsibilities may help you collaborate with the speech-language pathologist in a more comprehensive and intentional way. It may allow you to collaborate with increased focus and expanded knowledge, potentially resulting in greater positive impact for the young learners in your classroom and life. Let's begin our discussion by building knowledge of the field of speech-language pathology. Speech-language pathologists provide specialized speech and language assessment and intervention in a variety of settings, including long-term care, medical-based facilities, private practice, clinical settings, and schools, working with adults and children. The primary focus for the purpose of this book will be specific to speech-language pathologists working with children birth – eight years primarily in early childhood education school environments and homes. Speech-language pathologists, particularly in educational settings, are sometimes associated, almost exclusively at times, with improving the production of misarticulated speech sounds. In fact, speech sound disorders, including articulation disorders, phonological disorders, and childhood apraxia of speech, are an important focus in speech-language pathology practice; however, it is also important to gain knowledge and understanding of the comprehensive communication focus on assessment and intervention that includes the language domains of communication.

Language includes oral and written expression, listening and reading comprehension, and social pragmatics expanding the practice of speech-language pathologists well beyond the accurate production of speech sounds. The combined and overlapping components of speech and language provide a strong literacy foundation for children to build upon for academic participation and success, including reading and writing, enjoyable social interactions, and functional communication across various contexts and environments. It is important to note all modalities, including listening and reading comprehension and oral and written expression have a core foundation built upon language skills and abilities.

Communication for All

There is benefit in understanding the history of the credentialing entity and the process to obtain the Certificate of Clinical Competence (CCC) in the field of speech-language pathology in the United States of America, in order to gain a better understanding of the specialized assessment and intervention that speech-language pathologists may offer in collaboration with the early childhood collegial team, including parents and educators. The American Speech-Language-Hearing Association (ASHA), founded in 1925, is the nationally recognized professional credentialing body for the speech-language pathology field in the United States. ASHA advocates for communication as a human right. The ASHA mission focuses on accessible and effective communication for all individuals (ASHA, 1997–2020). ASHA provides support to speech-language pathologists through research specific to evidence-based practice and advocacy within the field. Now that we have explored the role of the speech-language pathologist and the history and mission of ASHA, we are ready to begin a more in-depth look at the speech and language acquisition and development of our young learners, with a focus on the birth to eight years old timeframe.

Speech

Speech is an area of communication that we consider within the development of the overall communication system. It is one area of focus in the field of speech-language pathology and is an important component of effective communication. Speech encompasses the articulation or the production of speech sounds, the phonological patterns of the speech sound system, and the fluency of speech production. Have you ever found yourself concerned about your inability to understand your child or a child in your classroom or care? Or, perhaps, you noticed a few speech sound errors; "**w**abbit" for "**r**abbit," "**th**ink" for "**s**ink," or "**d**od" for "**d**og"? Maybe parents have asked you if they should be concerned about their child who substitutes the /p/ sound for the /f/ sound in the articulation of the word, "**p**an" for "**f**an." You may already identify the speech-language pathologist as the professional who can support and provide intervention with the goal of improving a child's production of these or other speech sound errors to improve speech clarity, also referred to as *intelligibility*. Intelligibility is a measure of how much speech is understood by the listener during a communication exchange.

I want to delve into the speech clarity component of communication with more specificity because, like all communication, there is a level of complexity in how speech-language pathologists analyze speech sound production. Speech clarity can be measured at various levels, including the production of a sound in isolation, at the syllable level, within a word in the initial, medial, or final positions, in a phrase or sentence, and in spontaneous conversation or connected speech. Intelligibility is often quantified with a somewhat subjective percentage that provides a measurement of speech clarity in specific contexts and at specified levels. For example, I might state a child whom I am providing intervention to due to a diagnosis of a speech sound delay is approximately 60 percent intelligible in conversation with a familiar listener. Let's break that information down and explain what each of the components of that statement offer to the overall understanding of the child's speech clarity. The statement identifies the child's overall clarity of speech as equal to 60 percent at the conversation level. This means the child is understood 60 percent of the time at the conversation level, but the listener is also specified. In this case, it is stated this is with a familiar listener, meaning the individual listener may be familiar with the child's error patterns, substitutions, or omissions, and may have relevant context supporting the ability to understand the expressed verbal communication. It is possible that the child would have a decreased percentage of overall speech clarity with an unfamiliar listener.

In my role as a speech-language pathologist, I consider the articulation of the various speech sounds in each word position, including initial, medial, and final. In some cases, a child may correctly articulate a speech sound in the final position of a word but misarticulate the sound in the initial position of a word or any combination of the word positions. It is often beneficial to determine if a child is able to articulate a sound correctly at any level and in any position at the word level. It is also important to note that speech sounds may often be impacted by the sounds around them, which may impact overall speech clarity. It is also important to consider the complexity of the production. Was the word a single or multisyllabic word? Did the word include vowel changes, such as "d**a**da" compared to "d**a**ddy"? Vowel changes may also increase the complexity of words. As a speech-language pathologist, I provide assessment and intervention for various speech sounds in various word positions of words and across different contexts. It is important to note, intelligibility often varies depending on the knowledge of the conversation context, as well as the familiarity of the listener with the child communicator. Intelligibility is based on a perceptual judgement related to the ability to understand a speaker's spontaneous speech. Often, increased intelligibility is observed or reported with a familiar listener and a known context. In my clinical experience, I have observed many occasions when parents and caregivers often understand their child's speech better than others because they are likely to anticipate their child's needs, adapt to specific speech sound errors, and are often more likely to be aware of the context of the communication message.

Speech Sound Development Ages and Stages

Let's continue to investigate the *speech* area of communication and the role it plays in communication by exploring developmental milestones and the progression of acquisition and development during the early childhood years. We know sounds are combined to form words, words are combined to form sentences, and sentences are combined to form conversation or written expression. Understanding this process of sound, word, and sentence combination leads us to the starting point, specifically individual speech sounds. Individual speech sounds, also referred to as phonemes, combine to form words. We aren't referring to the orthographic letters or the alphabetic principle of speech sound connection to orthography, but instead, we are exploring the actual speech sound produced. These individual speech sounds are absent of meaning when produced in isolation. When we say the sound /p/, no meaning exists, but when we say /p/ within the word "pan," the word represents the item we use to cook. The combination of individual speech sounds into words provides us meaningful units within the communication system we use daily across multiple and varied interactions. Exploration of individual speech sounds combining to form words brings us to the discussion of developmental milestones specific to the acquisition and mastery of the production of individual speech sounds that impact overall speech clarity and effective, functional communication.

Developmental milestones and trajectories are important for determining why and how children should progress with speech and language development. Researchers have published speech and language milestones to guide us in determining if a child is following a typical and timely developmental trajectory. Keep in mind developmental milestones have ranges and that each individual infant, toddler, and child will develop at different rates. It is important to note that speech sounds develop over the course of the early childhood years. Speech sounds are not acquired all at one time or in a single moment of development. Shriberg (1993) conducted a study that resulted in a three-stage developmental model of speech sound acquisition in young children providing insight into when sounds are expected to develop. He suggested early (/m, b, j, n, w, d, p, h/), middle (/t, ŋ, k, g, f, v, tʃ, dʒ/) and late sounds (/ʃ, θ, s, z, ð, l, r, ʒ/). Table 2.1, developed based on Shriberg's (1993) model of speech sound acquisition, provides the specified early, middle, and late sounds. Table 2.1 provides an example of a word for each speech sound specified. It is important to note that the sound is only represented in a single word position for the purpose of examples within the table. The

TABLE 2.1
Speech Sound Acquisition

Early (expected by age 3 years)	Middle (expected by age 6 years)	Late (expected by age 8 years)
/m/ "mama"	/t/ "top"	/ʃ/ "ship"
/b/ "baby"	/ŋ/ "ring"	/θ/ "think"
/j/ "yes"	/k/ "key"	/s/ "sink"
/n/ "no"	/g/ "go"	/z/ "zoo"
/w/ "win"	/f/ "five"	/ð/ "the"
/d/ "dog"	/v/ "van"	/l/ "look"
/p/ "papa"	/tʃ/ "chip"	/r/ "rake"
/h/ "hat"	/dʒ/ "jam"	/ʒ/ "measure"

Shriberg (1993).

International Phonetic Alphabet (IPA) symbols are used to represent the speech sound or phoneme represented in each word.

Several research studies, including Sander (1972), Templin (1957), and Wellman, Case, Mengert, and Bradbury (1931) provide additional resources for determining the chronological age at which individual speech sounds should be acquired and produced with 75 percent or 90 percent accuracy dependent upon the study. Based on the studies, children should acquire and master /p, b, m, n, h, w/ by three years old; /d, k, g, f, y/ by four years old; /t, ŋ, r, l/ by six years old; and /s, z, v, ð, ʒ/ by eight years old. I offer these multiple research studies found in the literature to provide insight into the similarities and additional information offered among and across studies related to speech sound development during the early childhood years. Note that in the summarized literature, all speech sounds are expected to reach a level of mastery by age eight years, which aligns with our discussion of speech and language acquisition and development during the early childhood years, specifically birth through eight years.

In discussing individual speech sounds and production mastery, it is important to understand that a child may be able to say individual sounds in isolation, outside of the context of a word, with accuracy; however, when combining speech sounds into words, phrases, sentences, or connected speech may experience decreased speech sound production accuracy, resulting in decreased intelligibility. Overall intelligibility is an important developmental marker for monitoring speech sound development and progress because clarity of speech has the potential to positively or negatively impact effectiveness of communication exchanges. It is important to note that speech intelligibility is not a measure of intelligence or cognition, but instead is a measure of how well an individual is understood by the listening communication partner. Weiss (1982) offers percentages of typical speech intelligibility expected specific to chronological age to guide us in determining how intelligible a child is expected to be at a specific age, including 26–50 percent by 2 years old, 51–70 percent by 2 years; 6 months, and 71–80 percent by 3 years old.

Phonology

In addition to the acquisition of individual speech sounds, phonology is an important component of speech sound production. Phonology focuses on the speech sound system and patterns. We will explore phonological awareness in a later chapter highlighting the important connection to literacy, including reading, spelling, and writing. For the purposes of this portion of this chapter's discussion, we will explore phonology in relation to speech sound patterns and phonological processes linked to speech clarity. Phonological processes are a part of the typical speech sound developmental process. These phonological processes offer simplification of words to aid in the early production of words as young children are learning to sequence sounds into words when they are beginning to talk. Just as we discussed with the individual speech sound acquisition in regards to following a typical developmental trajectory, phonological processes also follow a specified progression. For the purpose of overall general knowledge specific to phonological systems, I have included phonological processes disappearing by three years of age and those disappearing after age three years to highlight when these processes are expected during development. I have included examples of the various phonological processes that are common during early childhood development. Tables 2.2 and 2.3 were developed to outline some of the more common phonological

TABLE 2.2
Phonological Processes Disappearing by Age 3 Years

Phonological Processes (Disappear by Age 3 Years)	Example
Unstressed Syllable Deletion	"nana" for "banana"
Final Consonant Deletion	"bu" for "bug"
Diminutization	"piggie" for "pig"
Velar Fronting	"tar" for "car"
Consonant Assimilation	"dod" for "dog"
Prevocalic Voicing	"van" for "fan"
Reduplication	"wawa" for "water"

Stoel-Gammon and Dunn (1985) and Bowen (2011).

TABLE 2.3
Phonological Processes Persisting after Age 3 Years

Phonological Processes (Persist after Age 3 Years)	Example
Cluster Reduction	"poon" for "spoon"
Epenthesis	"pu-lay" for "play"
Gliding	"wed" for "red"
Vowelization	"botto" for "bottle"
Stopping	"pan" for "fan"
Depalatization	"dit" for "dish"
Final Devoicing	"back" for "bag"

Stoel-Gammon and Dunn (1985) and Bowen (2011).

processes; however, this is not an exhaustive list and should not be used as such. Additionally, we must always consider that each child is an individual and it is important to remember that some children may not demonstrate any or all of the phonological processes listed. When specific phonological processes persist beyond the expected developmental age range, a consideration of a speech sound screening or comprehensive speech sound assessment may result, particularly if these phonological errors negatively impact a child's speech clarity and ability to engage in effective communication exchanges. The latest phonological process of gliding may persist until a child is six to seven years old.

Although phonological processes may persist beyond age three years, all phonological processes should disappear by seven years old (Shipley & McAfee, 2016).

Fluency

The final area of speech acquisition and development we need to explore is fluency. Fluency is the flow and continuity of speech. The important information to include specific to fluency and speech development is related to normal disfluency during the typical speech and language development trajectory. Perhaps your child or a child in your classroom has exhibited disfluent speech. The child may experience disfluent speech when beginning a word or sentence, including repetition of the initial sound or word. For example, "I-I-I want to play with the car." Additionally, a child may utilize fillers, such as "um" or "uh." For example, "um-um-um, can I ride my scooter now." Children may experience some level of disfluent speech during the preschool years as a result of a fast growing vocabulary combined with overall language development with sentence structure, social interactions, and various word forms. For the purpose of our discussion in this chapter related to development, it is important to note that disfluencies may be a part of the typical speech development trajectory, as speech and language are developing.

Sound Systems across Languages

Additionally, it is important when considering the milestones and trajectory of speech sound development that we gain increased knowledge and understanding that speech sounds development along differing developmental trajectories dependent upon each child's primary language. Sounds develop at different ages dependent on when the specific sounds are expected to develop in the child's primary spoken language and sound inventories vary across languages. I encourage you to keep in mind that the focus of the speech sound development information that I have provided is specific to children speaking English as their first language. In working with monolingual children who speak English and bilingual and multilingual children who speak English as a second or third language, I embrace the need to engage in ongoing work in building my cultural competency and knowledge of the primary languages of the children and families that I work with in clinical practice. I don't speak the first language of all the children I work with, but I do work to build my cultural awareness and competence to support building strong speech and language foundations for each child and collaborative interactions with families. Speech-language pathologists utilize various resources to determine the developmental trajectory for each child's first language. In Chapter 6 we will discuss the importance of diagnosis and eligibility, as well as the reasons for ensuring speech sound assessment is grounded in the child's primary spoken language. Children who are bilingual or for whom English is not their primary spoken language need to be assessed using the norms and milestones associated with his or her primary language.

Language

We have now built a foundation for understanding speech development. Let's continue our conversation with a discussion of the *language* area of communication. Remember, I mentioned that although speech-language pathologists might be frequently associated with intervention related to speech sound acquisition, development, and production mastery, they are also a key team member in supporting a young child's language acquisition and development. As we navigate the complexity of each communication exchange, it is important to consider both expressive and receptive language modalities. Since both are important for effective communication, communication breakdowns often occur if there is a deficit in either or both communication modalities. *Receptive language*, also known as language comprehension, is the ability to understand what is said to us. This area includes skills such as, pointing to pictures, following single and multi-step directions, and understanding questions, including yes/no and wh-questions, including *what, who, when,* and *where*. We also need to consider reading comprehension as young children begin exploring the meaning of written text in the early elementary school years as a component of receptive language. *Expressive language* is our language output, including sharing ideas, communicating emotions, naming items, and forming grammatically accurate sentences. It is important to identify and revisit the nonverbal and verbal methods of expressively communicating, including body language, gestures, and facial expressions. Written expression is also a mode of language output we must consider as a young child moves into the early elementary years with the introduction of writing. These examples of expressive and receptive language are not exhaustive, but instead provide a framework for understanding the types of communication tasks associated with each area. Both areas of language are equally important to the success of a communication exchange between communication partners. A breakdown in either expressive or receptive language may result in an ineffective reciprocal communication exchange or the inability to sustain a quality communication encounter.

Language can be summarized at a basic level into three distinct areas, including *form*, *content*, and *use* (Bloom & Lahey, 1978). The *form* of language includes sound patterns (phonology), the forms of words (morphology), and the rules for combining words and sentences (syntax). The *content* of language includes the vocabulary and word meaning comprising our communication exchanges (semantics). Finally, the *use* of language includes the social components and context of language (pragmatics). These areas of language working together simultaneously build a comprehensive and effective communication experience. Identifying and understanding these areas and the associated language domains can assist us in determining the what, why, and how of communication breakdowns. This information can also aid us in supporting the acquisition and development of skills within each of these important areas of language.

Language Acquisition: The Early Years

The acquisition of language during the early childhood years begins with the prelinguistic stage occurring before a child's first true word is spoken. This stage includes reflexive and nonreflexive vocalizations. During the prelinguistic stage of language acquisition, the sounds produced lack true meaning. During early infancy, reflexive sounds such as burps and cries occur. Oller (1980) stated that all babies go through the specific stages of prelinguistic development outlined in this paragraph. We will explore each stage and develop a basis for understanding how these early vocal developmental phases lead to the eventual production of an infant's first true word, usually occurring around the infant's first birthday. During the initial stage, the *Phonation Stage*, an infant produces reflexive vocalizations, such as crying or burping. It should be noted these sounds often sound similar to vowel and nasal sounds. The *Coo and Good Stage* follows at approximately two to three months of age when an infant begins to produce vowels and short consonant-vowel syllable structures. During this stage, the infant is now beginning to practice vocalizations that move sound productions towards consonant sounds. The next stage, *Exploration and Expansion*, usually occurring around four to six months, includes increased vocal play. Infants begin to squeal or make raspberries, with beginning consonant-vowel sound productions. The *Canonical Babbling Stage*, at seven to nine months, begins to include reduplicated babbling sequences and some vowel changes in the sequences. For example, an infant may babble "mama" (reduplicated babbling) and "mamo" (vowel change or variegated babbling). The final prelinguistic stage before the first word is the *Jargon Stage*, occurring around 10 to 12 months of age. During this stage, an infant begins to vocalize intonation patterns similar to those used in sentences and there is continued and significant growth of consonant and vowel productions. It is important to remember that although there are often specific chronological ages associated with various developmental stages and milestones, these stages do not occur in isolation and often occur with some overlap of the various aspects of sound development.

As infants approach their first birthday, meaningful words begin to emerge and a transition out of the babbling stage occurs. Infants continue to acquire additional words with typically a 15-word vocabulary by 15 months (Stoel-Gammon & Dunn,

1985). It never ceases to intrigue me in my study of child language when I consider the significant increase in the number of words and the increased language complexity developed during these early stages. Children begin to vocalize two-word phrases around the time their vocabulary reaches 50 words, generally at approximately 18 months. As they begin to explore with two-word phrases, we often hear telegraphic speech that communicates a message but in a simplified form; such as "more juice" to request more juice during snack. Language continues to expand and grow with increasing sentence length and complexity, including the use of action and descriptive words during the preschool and early elementary years.

Supporting Early Language Development

If you are an early childhood educator during these early stages of language acquisition, you have the opportunity to be part of the time in a young child's life that I view as one that is full of excitement and teachable moments. I have been afforded the opportunity to spend time in many early childhood education and development settings, both homes and schools, during my career. The opportunity to observe the ongoing support of language acquisition continues to be a joyful observation. Watching language grow and flourish in the naturalistic environments provided by the early childhood years always leaves me reflecting on ways to continue to enhance these opportunities for our young learners within these valuable language rich environments. I want to ask you to pause for a moment to reflect on the amazing role you play in a child's communication foundation. Have you truly ever taken the time to realize the valuable and irreplaceable role you play in these early childhood language development opportunities? Parents, early childhood educators, caregivers, and siblings, to name only a few, have the opportunity each day to model and encourage language development and growth with our youngest learners. The early childhood home and education environments are exciting places filled with so many language opportunities!

I want to offer some ideas for supporting language acquisition and continued development that I have used over the course of my professional clinical career as a speech-language pathologist in school-based early education programs, early intervention in home environments, and private practice clinical settings. I want to encourage you to consider ways to build upon the excellent language opportunities already found in your language-rich home or classroom setting. A great starting point is as simple as talking with a child. At the most basic level, when we talk with young children we are providing language input and encouraging opportunities for reciprocal communication. In the earliest infant months, infants begin to perceive the rhythm and intonation of language, engage in eye contact, and reciprocal vocalizations. Have you experienced an infant vocalizing vowel sounds in response to you? Perhaps the infant vocalizations appeared to mimic your intonation? The prosody, intonation, or stress on various sounds or syllables are often imitated by infants and young children even from the earliest speech and language development stages. The development of language begins with the suprasegmental aspects, including intonation, prosody, and stress. As we continue to explore the way talking provides important language input for young language learners, I want to point you to a few key aspects of talking that I have identified in my years of clinical practice. We want to talk **with** not **at** or **to** young children. What do I mean by this statement? When communicating with young children, we need to pause and account for several considerations. One of the most difficult that I have observed with others, and find personally challenging at times, is pausing to provide time for a child to respond. In communication exchanges, the pace is often fast with changing topics, multiple communication partners, and long, complex sentences running together. Children need time to process language and respond at their individual level of language understanding and expression, particularly during early language development.

I want to explore a scenario that presents some potential language challenges, as well as provide ideas for supporting language development and use in similar scenarios. Have you ever asked a young child an open-ended question, such as "What did you do today at school?" or "What would you like to tell us about your vacation this summer?" only to receive complete silence or a shoulder shrug in response? I'm sure many can relate to this moment. You might be asking yourself why this happens because there are so many ways to respond to these questions and so much potential for a reciprocal communication exchange opportunity, right? Yes, in fact, that is true, and you are accurate in your assessment. There are a multitude of accurate answers and generally a large amount of information that could be communicated to initiate and sustain a substantial reciprocal communication exchange. So why doesn't it always result in a positive and successful, reciprocal communication exchange with a young child? Believe me, I have experienced similar situations, and, over the years, I have explored, tried, and shared options for improving these situations for children and their communication partners. I want to explore this a little further in the upcoming *Communication Connection*. Take some time to explore and discuss the scenario outlined. Reflect on the connection to the practical application of communication strategies.

COMMUNICATION CONNECTION

Consider a time when you have asked a young child an open-ended question. What was the question you asked and what were the specific situation details? Were you in the car, at home, or in the classroom? Were there other people joining in the conversation? Consider the following questions related to your specific scenario to analyze how providing language models and support could enhance the communication exchange and build additional language learning opportunities. Below each question I have provided an explanation of why these questions may be important to consider when a communication breakdown occurs.

1. **What was the question you asked and what response did you receive?**

It is important to understand that although asking open-ended questions can open an opportunity for lengthy, complex, and descriptive communication, it can also leave a young child unsure of what information is important to share. This may be a particularly relevant consideration during the early language learning years when children are acquiring and learning the most effective use of language. When asking a child, "What did you do at school today?" we open the door for a multitude of answers, but we also aren't providing a clear understanding of what information should be communicated based on importance and relevancy. Additionally, when asking a question such as the one in this example, think of all the events that happen in a day at school and all the accompanying components. If someone asks you about your day at work, how do you approach it? I can only speak from my personal experience and my response to this question. I would guess that, like me, many might focus on the successful highlights and perhaps talk and process through some of the challenges of the day. We typically don't outline each and every detail of the day from beginning to end. That approach would take an inordinate amount of time and, generally speaking, most of us likely would have difficulty recalling every aspect of the entire day. In addition, outlining each detail of a given day may result in decreased attention or topic maintenance with your communication partner. As established language users with strong, intact communication systems, we can determine the most important aspects and relevant details to share. Now let's revisit our young language learner who likely isn't sure what information would be relevant to share and let's be honest, sharing it *all* seems like a daunting task. It is always fun to meet a child who is asked this very question and shares every detail from arrival at school to departure. It is even more fun to see the adult's reaction. They often act surprised with all the information, but I often provide a gentle reminder of "you asked the question." It is important to remember that, as a young language learner, it can be difficult at times to discern the information that is most relevant to share with communication partners.

2. **If you asked the question and received silence in response, how did you respond? Did you ask more questions? Did you abandon the attempt?**

    Let's set the stage for this interaction. You pick up your young child after work. It has been a busy and long day, but you are very interested in hearing about your child's day at school. You are driving home and ask the big picture question, "What did you do at school today?" Your question is met with the long silent pause. I should admit right now that the silent pause is difficult for me. Do you ever find the pause uncomfortable? I always want to fill it with words. I am a speech-language pathologist so talking is definitely more comfortable than long pauses for me! Filling long pauses with words isn't necessarily the wrong approach, but I want to offer a few suggestions for how to fill that space in a meaningful way to model language for framing the current interaction and planting seeds for future communication exchanges.

    First, try not to abandon the communication attempt. Opportunities like these are teachable moments and I am always motivated to find fun and creative ways to build language development and use into any and all moments. You can approach this scenario in a variety of ways based on the situation and individual child's need. I am going to outline a few options that I have used successfully with young language learners. I want to encourage you to realize that there is no right answer, no one-size-fits-all, when using strategies and tools to build and grow effective communication. Find a strategy that is most effective and comfortable for you and your young child. Keep in mind that the strategy will likely differ when considering various communication scenarios and young communicators. Different strategies may work in different situations

or with different communication partners. The following strategies have been successful during my clinical practice in communicating with young language learners.
A. Ask questions to narrow the topic and provide guidance for establishing relevant answers. Suggestions related to our question about the day's events at school might include, "What did you eat for afternoon snack?" "Did you go outside to play?" "What story book did your teacher read during circle time today?" These questions provide direction for the reciprocal communication exchange giving the young communicator specific starting points to identify relevant information. They also are likely to provide you with additional details resulting in follow-up questions, building increased back-and-forth reciprocal exchange, to build and sustain the initiated conversation. As a speech-language pathologist, increased reciprocal communication circles or back-and-forth exchanges are exciting stuff! These reciprocal exchanges build social language skills, including, turn-taking, topic maintenance, topic expansion, and sustained conversation skills.
B. After reading the above suggestion, you might be thinking, that sounds great, but I tried that option, and I am still being met with the long, uncomfortable silence. I would continue to encourage you not to abandon this language-learning opportunity when possible. This is an excellent moment for language modeling. You might begin by asking, "Guess what I did at work today?" followed by answers to that question broken down in a way that highlights relevant information. I often will ask the larger, open-ended question listed, but then will break it down with more narrow questions accompanied by the answers. An example of this strategy might be, "Would you like to know what I had for lunch today?" followed by a short pause and the answer, "I had some chicken

and rice." Depending on the child, you might add in some details about forgetting your fork and needing to eat your chicken and rice with a spoon. These guided questions and answers sometimes will lead the child to ask you follow-up questions. Or another favorite strategy of mine that has worked with so many young language learners I have interacted with: after modeling this question and answer, I will then circle back around and ask, "Do you remember what you ate for lunch today?" With a model of finding and communicating the relevant information, a child will often respond to the question with an accurate answer. This can become a back-and-forth exchange with you *modeling* and guiding the communication. While it is exciting to see this strategy work, I want to emphasize the important way you are building practice and understanding of these types of communication exchanges, including identifying relevant information and details and understanding and answering a variety of questions. You are providing a language model for future communication and allowing practice with a trusted communication partner during the early language development years.

C. Although this final strategy is one I will often use with children experiencing more significant challenges with the form, content, and use of language, this strategy can also be utilized successfully with children acquiring language, as well as, learning how to effectively use communication during the early childhood years. I have helped teachers and parents develop a simple communication system that provides the parent or teacher with information. The parent will provide details of home events and the teacher will do the same for school events. This can be done in so many creative ways depending on preferred communication modes. Consider a communication notebook, email, a phone call, or text. The purpose is to provide both the teacher and parent with details to support effective communication exchanges with the child. It is easy to ask questions and help a child communicate an answer effectively if you know the answer ahead of time. For example, if a family was on vacation at a beach, it is much easier to guide a detailed discussion of the time at the beach with the young child if a teacher has a few of the details ahead of time. It also limits the need to abandon a communication attempt because little to no support can be offered without relevant details. In addition, it minimizes the possibility of filling in gaps with potentially inaccurate details, which may be confusing to the child.

3. **Revisit the scenario you outlined for this Communication Connection. What was effective? Are there considerations that may enhance this type of communication attempt in the future?**
Would you change the way you modeled language during the communication exchange? If not, what effective strategies did you utilize and why did they work? If you would choose to model in a different way, what strategy would you utilize? Why would you choose that particular approach? How would you highlight the relevant details within the framework of the big picture question?

This *Communication Connection* provides a single example of how *talking with* young language learners has the potential to plant seeds for future effective communication. Modeling is an effective strategy for providing young children opportunities to hear language and build an understanding of how it is constructed and used. Additional strategies for supporting language acquisition during the early childhood years include expansion and extension. Think of expansion as simply building onto a child's utterance without adding any additional or new information. Extensions also build on a young child's utterance, but they add new information to the child's expression. In the examples listed below, I have provided ways to expand an utterance and then extend it providing new information. Both provide models to support language growth, but note the differences in the way the language models provide information. The best part about modeling, expansion, and extension is that these strategies can be used in any situation and natural environment. These strategies are an excellent way to support all language learners, regardless of a typical language development trajectory, a language delay, or a language disorder. I have encouraged teachers to utilize these strategies in the classroom, on the playground, and in the lunchroom to name a few. For parents, these strategies can be great in the grocery store, in the car, on the playground, or during everyday routines, such as meal time. The key is to find activities or routines that encourage a child to express using gestures, signs, words, or individual communication modalities based on the child's strengths and needs, within daily routines occurring in the natural environment. Once the child is using expressive language, the opportunities to use language expansions and extensions are robust and, most importantly, the child and adult can experience the joy of playing and communicating for sustained periods of time. Additionally, these strategies can be utilized in the classroom with groups of children. The same technique applies because you are simply modeling expanded forms of utterances or you are providing the group of children an extension of information to enhance language growth. It is important to note that when I am utilizing expansion and extensions, I don't require the child to respond. I am simply utilizing these strategies to input language. Some children may imitate or also offer an expansion or extension. Language output is excellent and always welcome but is not a requirement of these language learning opportunities. I want to emphasize again that these strategies are relevant and beneficial to all language learners.

Expressing language through interactions including verbalizations, gestures, and signs is my favorite way to build language, but sliding in as a close second is found in my love of books, specifically children's literature. Reading and interacting, in an intentional way, with children's literature is one of my favorite activities to engage with young children. I love books and the

TABLE 2.4
Language Expansion and Extension

Child's Utterance	Expansion	Extension
More juice	You want more juice.	You want more juice. You are thirsty.
Car go	Yes, the car is going.	The car is going up the track and over the hill.

excitement of sharing the fun of books with an infant or child opens so many doors for those teachable language moments, including naming pictures, pointing to pictures, modeling grammatical structures of language, asking and answering questions, story recall and sequencing, and vocabulary development to name only a few. As children begin to read and write, they are offered models of written text and opportunities for reading comprehension, adding to their language expression and comprehension skills through additional modalities. Intentionally interacting with books goes far beyond just reading the words on the page. In fact, with young children, I often don't start with reading the words on the page. I tell the story using the pictures and ask the child to identify objects or actions by pointing. As children progress, I might have them help me "guess what might happen next" or "tell me what is happening in the picture." These are additional opportunities for me to encourage expressive communication, model language components and grammatical structures, build vocabulary, and increase background knowledge. Classrooms and homes are often filled with books and children often demonstrate an interest in books that opens a door for a fantastic language learning opportunity. I'm also certain that many of us have experienced a child's enthusiasm about reading the same book over and over again. How many children's books do you have memorized because you have read them to a child so many times? So many come to mind for me! The simple act of reading to children introduces them to vocabulary, sentence structure, and the rhythm of language. We can also use books to build identification and naming skills. Additionally, we can engage in reciprocal communication exchanges involving asking and answering questions, introducing children to question forms, including yes/no, what, who, where, when, and why. As children develop more language skills, we can begin to ask them to sequence stories and retell them using their words. Children often will pick repetitive books that include a specific phrase repetition or sequence of events and ask to read you the story. My favorite part of this activity is when the child begins to embellish the story with new imagined details they generate, providing evidence of their creative thinking and growing language skills. It is the perfect example of the child *extending* language and also building confidence in the communication process and feeling empowered to share individual thoughts and ideas!

Language: Moving into the Primary School Years

As children move into the early primary school years, vocabulary continues to grow and principles of reading begin to be introduced. It is important to consider the impact of continued emphasis on background knowledge and the importance of vocabulary. We will discuss additional information related to vocabulary and phonological awareness in Chapter 4. One aspect I want to discuss related to our discussion of the primary school years is the introduction of specific academic language. As children move into kindergarten, there are varying degrees of exposure to the school environment, social interactions, large group instruction, and knowledge of the procedures of the various components of a school day. Regardless of a child's prior exposure to school and social experiences, the move into kindergarten is a substantial transition, both for the child and parents.

Learning the procedures and routines is a large part of the transition to kindergarten. Perhaps children are attending school for the first time or a full day program is introduced for the first time. I have been part of first days of kindergarten on many occasions in my years of clinical practice. There is often a combination of excitement, tears, and, at times, confusion about the expectations. Children need to continue the navigation of interpersonal interactions, as well as the academic language associated with the primary school years. The visual and narrative nature of the early primary years is supportive of the continued language learning environment. Early elementary school educators often provide visual cues, using pictures, pointing, gestures, combined with narration and song to support language learning. My work as a speech-language pathologist has allowed me to see firsthand the positive impact of providing visual support during the early elementary years. These supports offer additional contextual cues, as well as a multimodal approach to learning that will benefit all the young learners in a classroom.

As we continue to explore the early elementary education years in a young language learner's life, it is important to remember that oral language, including vocabulary and grammatical knowledge, is correlated to the literacy components of reading and writing (Lonigan & Shanahan, 2008). This highlights the importance of the oral language foundation built during the early years and the impact of strong oral language skill development on the future development of reading, writing, and spelling. Although this isn't new information, it is important to reiterate to support the essential language foundation built during a child's early language learning years. As a young child enters elementary school, we need to pause for a moment and attempt to look through the lens of the child, including recognition of the new routines, increased complexity of directions, introductions to expressive language in written formats, decoding and reading comprehension, and a need for building increased independence in navigating the world. These are not small tasks! We need to consider young children who enter kindergarten with a small vocabulary inventory, reduced background knowledge based on experiences, a primary language other than English, reduced speech clarity resulting from speech sound errors, difficulty formulating sentences to convey ideas, or difficulty following directions with multiple steps. We support children and scaffold instruction to meet the needs and promote growth in young children with diverse and varied levels of communication abilities each day in elementary school classrooms. Scaffolded communication becomes a key part of classroom teaching in early elementary classrooms.

Vocabulary is a key factor of communication, combined with the background knowledge associated with various experiences. Taking the time to build and solidify a strong vocabulary base has the potential to support students in oral communication, reading comprehension, and written expression. I want to share an activity I have utilized often to support students in developing mental representations or pictures, as well as, to build a child's descriptive vocabulary inventory. I will describe an object to a young child and ask him or her to guess what I am thinking of after my description. For example, I am thinking of an animal that is soft, has whiskers, and says "meow," what am I thinking of? Hopefully, the child will respond "cat," or we can work to think through the descriptive components to help the child arrive at the answer. Once the child has developed a solid foundation in identification, I will then ask him or her to describe an object to me so that I can guess what the object is. It is a simple and fun game, but let's break down how it supports language, in the following ways: (1) the child is receiving input of descriptive words linked to a specific object or referent to build knowledge of descriptive vocabulary, (2) the child is processing the information and may develop a mental image that may potentially support reading comprehension, and (3) the child begins to use descriptive words building the complexity of oral communication with potential carryover to written communication. Additionally, shared book reading, text talks, and phonological awareness activities, such as rhyming, continue to build important vocabulary knowledge and phonemic awareness essential for reading comprehension, meaningful written expression, and oral communication. I believe the more opportunities children have to experience books, experiential learning opportunities, and communication exchanges the more skilled they will become. Like any activity, the more practice we have, the more likely we are to build our performance mastery. The early elementary years include an opportunity to continue to build the language base necessary for continued learning using oral expression, reading comprehension, and written expression. In Chapter 4, we will revisit the importance of vocabulary building and phonological awareness during the early childhood years, including the early elementary school years and identify strategies and activities focused on the development of these foundational skills. Before we explore these skills in more detail, we will discuss the relationship between the brain and the development of language in more detail in Chapter 3.

Bibliography

American Speech-Language-Hearing Association (1997–2020). About The American Speech-Language-Hearing Association (ASHA). Retrieved from www.asha.org [September 5, 2020].

Bloom, L. & Lahey, M. (1978). *Language Development and Language Disorders* (Wiley Series on Communication Disorders) 1st edition. Farmington Hills, MI: Macmillan.

Bowen, C. (2011). Table 3: Elimination of phonological processes. Retrieved from www.speech-language-therapy.com/ on [October 1, 2020].

Lonigan, C. & Shanahan, T. (2008). Executive summary of the report of the National Early Literacy Panel. Retrieved from https://lincs.ed.gov/publications/pdf/NELPReport09.pdf on [September 15, 2020].

Oller, D. K. (1980) The emergence of the sounds of speech in infancy. *Child Phonology*, 1, 93–112.

Sander, E. K. (1972). When are speech sounds learned?. *Journal of Speech and Hearing Disorders*, 37(1), 55–63.

Shipley, K. G., & McAfee, J. G. (2016). *Assessment in Speech-language Pathology: A Resource Manual*. Boston, MA: Cengage Learning.

Shriberg, Lawrence D. (1993). Four new speech and prosody-voice measures for genetics research and other studies in developmental phonological disorders. *Journal of Speech, Language, and Hearing Research*, 36(1), 105–140.

Stoel-Gammon, C. & Dunn, C. (1985). *Normal and Disordered Phonology in Children*. (Child Language Acquisition Series). Austin, TX: Pro ed.

Templin, M. (1957). *Certain Language Skills in Children: Their Development and Interrelationships*. Minneapolis, MN: University of Minnesota Press.

Weiss, C. E. (1982). *Weiss Intelligibility Test*. Tigard, OR: CC Publications.

Wellman, B., Case, I., Mengert, I., & Bradbury, D. (1931). Speech sounds of young children. *University of Iowa Study, Child Welfare*, 5(2), 1–82.

3

Brain Development and Language

Identifying Historical and Landmark Perspective

As we continue to explore expressive and receptive language within natural environments, including homes and classrooms, I find it necessary to pause and remind ourselves of the historical perspectives and landmark researchers providing significant contributions to the ongoing study of speech and language acquisition and development. The theoretical constructs provide the foundation for the continued discussion of speech, language, and learning. Although I don't personally believe you are required to have a detailed and comprehensive understanding of each of these theories committed to memory, I believe the historical knowledge offered to us by lead researchers specific to cognitive, speech, and language development warrant a place in our discussion. You may be familiar with these theorists and researchers or this may be the first time you are being introduced to them. I hope you will embrace the opportunity to revisit perspectives and research familiar to you. Additionally, I hope you will explore and gain knowledge from the information provided about those researchers and theorists you may be less familiar with and consider the impact they have made on our study of speech, language, and cognitive development.

This chapter will offer a basic historical perspective of the contributions of Brown, Piaget, Chomsky, and Vygotsky. I want to emphasize the fact that additional researchers have contributed to the base of knowledge and continued discussion specific to speech and language acquisition and development. The purpose of this chapter is not to develop a significant investigation or depth of understanding of the theories and research constructs; however, my review of the literature related to the theoretical research, linked to an ongoing exploration of speech and language development, has focused on the work of these landmark researchers contributing to this body of work. Other authors, researchers, theorists, and practitioners may focus their study on other historical perspectives based on the work of other theorists and researchers. I am choosing to discuss those listed because I find their work particularly related, significant, and interesting to my work.

The purpose of the historical perspective, found within this book, is to provide a starting point for our discussion of the research and theoretical foundations supporting the study of language and speech acquisition and development. If this information sparks your interest and desire to learn more about the work of these researchers and their classic work and findings, I encourage you to continue accessing and reviewing additional sources for ongoing investigation and study. I find great value in reviewing and understanding the research and underlying theoretical constructs of language and speech development to support identification and implementation of key strategies for building optimal communication environments and supporting children experiencing communication breakdowns. My motivation to build a strong and growing understanding of the most effective ways to support literacy development, create opportunities for effective communication practice and growth, and my love of the study of early childhood, particularly speech and language development, push me to continue to learn more about the brain, the impact of the environment, and the components of development.

The interesting consideration in discussing these researchers and theorists is that there are both complementary discussions and varying theories. These robust and ongoing theoretical discussions have continued to intrigue me and lead to a deeper review of the literature and inquiry about brain development and its relationship to the acquisition and development of language in children. At the most basic level of understanding, language acquisition and development research include the discussion of nature, the biological internal wiring, and nurture, the environmental stimuli and contexts. Dependent upon the theoretical construct and accompanying theorist, nature and nurture may surface as isolated discussion points or may result in an interacting paradigm with specified innate language components, combined with environmental influences and interactions.

Brain development and research is intriguing and complex in so many ways. It is particularly intriguing to me because of the connection to speech and language development. Our discussion of speech, language, and overall communication function in the previous chapters identified the complexity of communication, including speech sound production, language expression, and language understanding, as it relates to overall functional communication interactions. It is no surprise that the brain development, function, and theoretical constructs supporting language acquisition, development, and learning are also complex. It is evident as we look at the developmental trajectory of speech and language skills during a child's early years that speech and language development occur at an astonishingly rapid rate during the early childhood years, with skills developing simultaneously, building a speech and language foundation that supports the ongoing skill development necessary for effective and functional communication. As we explored in Chapter 2, speech and language development begins in the early childhood years and extends through the school years, and into adulthood.

Speech and language growth and development encompasses speech and all language domains, including the form, content, and use. Vocabulary inventories grow at a rapid rate, complexity and length of utterances expand, and language expression and comprehension extend to include written expression and reading comprehension as children develop. When I provide myself an opportunity to truly pause and consider the language acquisition and development process, I continue to be in awe of how rapidly young children develop an effective mode of expressive communication and the ability to comprehend language in a variety of contexts. As a speech-language pathologist, I am acutely aware of the way in which the use of language can appear simplistic, particularly when communication is functional and effective; however, I also realize the complexity of the components, language structures, and construction of language necessary for effective expression and comprehension of language. This complexity often becomes clear when there is a communication breakdown causing us to pause and consider what caused the ineffective communication exchange. I can't deny my ongoing intrigue and curiosity with the acquisition and development of speech and language. Understanding the science and theory provides a foundation for problem-solving and critical thinking when striving to build optimal communication environments for all communicators, as well as supporting mediation when communication breakdowns occur. I, along with many of you reading this book, know the importance of understanding the components and the processes for supporting ongoing language and literacy acquisition and development in children with typical language acquisition, as well as children in need of speech or language intervention, resulting from a delay or disorder. This understanding offers us a starting point to discuss various communication scenarios across many contexts, as well as the contributing researchers who have provided a foundation of knowledge.

Chomsky's Study of Syntax

I am going to begin our discussion with Noam Chomsky's Theory of Transformational Grammar, a central theory related to the nature perspective of language acquisition and development. Chomsky stated that humans have an innate set of language rules that allow an infinite number of utterances to be generated. Chomsky referred to the Language Acquisition Device (LAD) in his research, suggesting there is innate knowledge for the acquisition of any human language when an infant is exposed to the specific language (Chomsky, 1965). Additionally, Chomsky's Universal Grammar Theory suggested that developing young children have innate knowledge of specific characteristics of any language they are exposed to during language development, independent of sensory stimuli or experiences (Piaget, Chomsky, & Piattelli-Palmarini, 1980). Based on Chomsky's theory, this language information is stored in the LAD. If we consider the full realization of this theoretical construct, we must identify the underlying basis that a developing infant or young child would innately identify the relevant grammatical rules for the language being learned. Additionally, the child would develop a competency for utilizing these universal grammatical rules to formulate and understand an infinite number of novel utterances, focused primarily on the known grammatical rules, also referred to as the syntax of language. Chomsky's study of language acquisition and the identification of the LAD has the potential to explain the rapid and complex language acquisition of young children. Although a study of language acquisition may support the need for cognitive and perceptual knowledge, continued discussion of Chomsky's early theory is relevant to the influence of nature as part of early language and speech development.

Chomsky's continued study of the syntax of language introduced and expanded the conceptual and theoretical basis of universal grammar comprised of principles and parameters. Let's briefly delve into Chomsky's research to gain a stronger understanding of Universal Grammar. Chomsky's research provides the theoretical construct for the genetic component of language, identifying a universal set of rules innate to all humans absent of sensory experiences. Additionally, delving deeper into Chomsky's Universal Grammar, he stated individuals innately know principles that apply to all languages. Parameters are the finite rules that apply to a specific language. In summarizing Chomsky's research at a basic level of understanding connected to language acquisition, the principles shared by all languages are combined with parameters, specific to each individual language, to effectively construct and understand grammatically accurate language (Chomsky, 1993). Chomsky offered important and valuable insight and consideration of the consideration of innate components of language acquisition and development.

Brown's Study of Morphology

As we continue our discussion and investigation of language domains related to speech and language acquisition, I want to introduce another classic researcher, Roger Brown. Brown offers continued insight into syntax, the rules for combining words to form sentences, as well as morphology, a study of the structure and form of words. He focused on the use and complexity of expressive language. I am going to take us on a brief path of speech-language pathology talk for just a moment to offer some insight into one analysis that speech-language pathologists engage in to investigate word structure and syntactic complexity as it relates to language acquisition and effective use for functional communication. I am outlining this information to offer a framework of ways speech-language pathologists analyze language beyond the number of words used.

In the field of speech-language pathology we discuss and analyze free and bound morphemes. So, what is a morpheme? A morpheme is the smallest unit of language that holds meaning. Morphemes differ from speech sounds, also known as phonemes, because individual speech sounds do not hold meaning. Free morphemes are those units of language that can stand alone as words and hold meaning. Bound morphemes are units of language that can't stand alone but when bound to a free morpheme change the meaning of a word. These include prefixes and suffixes, which change meaning when they are bound to a word. Consider the meaning of the free morpheme "acceptable." Now, let's add a bound morpheme, "un," to "acceptable," resulting in the word, "unacceptable." The bound morpheme, when added to the free morpheme, changed the meaning of the word. Brown's research and accompanying findings offer stages of morphological and syntactic development, including five stages outlining the morphological structures expected to develop at each age. Brown's Mean Length of Utterance (MLU) analysis, utilizes language sampling to offer the speech-language pathologist a concrete method of analyzing morphology and syntax. How do speech-language pathologists use this information? Simply counting words does not always provide us with all the necessary information about the complexity of a young child's expressive language productions. Brown offers 14 grammatical morphemes to utilize in the analysis of morphological and syntactic language. Let's outline Brown's grammatical morphemes and consider an example of a child utterance to solidify this concept. Below you will find a summary of Brown's 14 grammatical morphemes outlined in the expected order of development. It should be noted that typical morphological development will include mastery of all morphemes by age four years. It is important when considering speech and language development that we understand we shouldn't operate in absolutes or isolation during analysis. Each young child is an individual and there are acceptable variations and ranges along the developmental trajectory, as well as variables across different settings. I don't provide this information with the expectation that you will collect and analyze a language sample but simply as a guide for considering the various morphological components of a young child's language learning that supports the increased length and complexity of a young child's functional communication. The purpose of this information is to provide you with a foundation for understanding the trajectory and progression of language acquisition to support your child or the children in your classroom on their language learning journey, as well as understand the purpose and process of collecting and analyzing a language sample completed by the speech-language pathologist. Additionally, you may find the information beneficial in identifying when a speech or language referral for screening or assessment may be warranted based on concerns of length and complexity of communication form or lack of grammatical morpheme use. Table 3.1 was developed based on Brown (1973) to provide examples of each of the grammatical morphemes.

TABLE 3.1
Morphology Development

Grammatical Morpheme	Example Utterance
Present Progressive -ing	The boy is go**ing**.
Prepositions in	Put the block **in** the box.
Preposition on	She put the spoon **on** the table.
Regular plural -s	The cat**s** are playing.
Irregular past tense verbs	The girl **ran** the race.
Regular possessive -s	This is the dog**'s** food.
Uncontractible copula	Where is she? There she **is**.
Articles a, an, the	**The** book is on the shelf.
Regular past tense -ed	The frog jump**ed** into the pond.
Regular third person -s	The rabbit hop**s** in the grass.
Irregular third person	He **has** a book about flowers.
Uncontractible auxiliary	She **was** singing.
Contractible copula	They**'re** going swimming tomorrow.
Contractible auxiliary	Mommy**'s** going for a walk with us.

Brown (1973).

Child Utterance Example
I going school.

Analysis
Counting the words in this example utterance is one way to analyze language expression. We can easily identify the three words the child produced: (1) I, (2) going, and (3) school. We can analyze that the child utilizes a subjective pronoun, a verb, and a noun. We may also note the child's utterance is simplified or missing an auxiliary verb form. Now, let's add an additional analysis step and consider the work of Brown (1973) related to morphological analysis. This utterance contains four morphemes: I, go, -ing, and school. If you recall, a morpheme is a meaningful unit of speech, therefore, -ing is a bound morpheme, which attaches to "go" and changes the verb tense to a present progressive form. This addition of "ing" changes the complexity of the child's expression because there is a use of the present progressive verb

tense. This is simply one example of how the analysis of morphological complexity works. Morphological analysis provides speech-language pathologists an additional measure to analyze a child's language expression to determine the complexity, as well as determine if the child is missing developmentally appropriate grammatical morphemes. Brown's research would tell us that we need a minimum of 50 to 100 utterances to complete a true language analysis, so the one example utterance provided would not offer the information necessary to gain a true and detailed morphological analysis. I simply wanted to provide a basic understanding of the additional information speech-language pathologists can acquire about the length and complexity of a child's language utilizing the findings of Roger Brown's research to highlight one of his contributions to the study of language acquisition and development.

Piaget's Study of Cognition and Language

Continuing with our investigation of the brain, language development, and the classic researchers informing our study, Jean Piaget's theory of cognitive development and associated language development introduced schemas, assimilations, and accommodations. Piaget provided a theoretical construct comprising four stages of cognitive development guiding continued discussion of language development. Piaget referenced children's environmental interactions in relation to support for their construction of language understanding. He emphasized the development of logical reasoning and thinking skills. Piaget's theory argued cognitive development is a combination of biological and environmental factors. Three significant, basic components are at the center of Piaget's Cognitive Theory, including schemas, the adaptation process, and cognitive developmental stages (Piaget & Claparède, 1959). Let's consider each of these components. First, Piaget discussed schemas, which are defined as the building blocks, providing knowledge to develop mental models of the surrounding world. The next component is the adaptation process. Think of this component as an adaptation to the building block or schema.

Assimilations and accommodations come into play within the adaptation process. Assimilations apply a known schema to deal with a current situation. Accommodations occur when a known schema does not successfully deal with a current situation, and, therefore, requires changing the schema to meet the needs of the new situation (Furth, Piaget, & Catholic University of America Department of Psychology, 1969). Young children utilize assimilations and accommodations to help navigate, make sense of, and interact with the world around them. Play-based scenarios are excellent opportunities to provide engagement and practice with assimilating and adapting to various changing schemas.

Now that we have established the first two components of Piaget's Cognitive Theory, we can outline the third component, Piaget's Stages of Cognitive Development. Based on his theory, each child is expected to experience each of the stages. Based on Piagetian Theory, development follows the same sequential order for each individual child. It is important to note that Piaget's research focused specifically on child development. He also focused his research on the developmental process, not the learning process, which differed from many researchers in the field.

Piaget outlined four stages, including the Sensorimotor Stage, Preoperational Stage, Concrete Operational Stage, and Formal Operational Stage (Furth, Piaget, & Catholic University of America Department of Psychology, 1969). The Sensorimotor Stage, occurring from birth to 18–24 months, focused on the development of object permanence. Object permanence requires the development of a mental schema of a given object to demonstrate awareness that an object still exists even when it has been hidden out sight. We often play games with infants and toddlers, showing an object and then hiding it under a blanket. A child with developed object permanence will demonstrate awareness of the object's existence even though it is hidden. Do you play peek-a-boo with infants? Did you know you are practicing object permanence? Have you ever hidden a ball under a blanket, and the infant lifts up the blanket, to see the ball and laughs at the game? Yes, you are practicing object permanence through play! As we continue to explore Piaget's Theory, we move to the Preoperational Stage occurring between two and seven years. During this stage, children continue to lack sophisticated perspective-taking of others; however, children think more symbolically so words and objects begin to represent something other than themselves. Have you ever watched a young child use a toy to represent another object? Perhaps the TV remote is used as a phone? A block is pushed around like a car? The toddler is beginning to explore the use of objects to represent other objects in the world. The Concrete Operational Stage introduces the beginning of logical thought and occurs during seven to 11 years. During this stage, children demonstrate a decreased need to actively work things out in the physical environment and are able to logically reason internally. Increased internal processing occurs as they continue to navigate their world. The final stage in Piaget's theoretical construct is the Operational Stage, occurring from 11 years to adulthood. During this ongoing stage, individuals develop the ability to logically consider abstract thoughts. Piaget's Cognitive Theory offers insight into the combination of building blocks of knowledge and environmental interactions. Additionally, when we consider the ages of each of Piaget's stages, the importance of the foundational sensorimotor and preoperational stages during the early childhood years for a child's development of logical and abstract thinking and reasoning in the concrete operational and operational stages becomes evident.

Vygotsky's Study of Social Interactions and Language

The last classical theorist I will introduce and include for the purposes of this book is Lev Vygotsky. Much of my theoretical study of language development and the learning process in the past several years has centered on the work of Vygotsky. Vygotsky introduced sociocultural theory based on cognitive development through social interactions into the language development arena. The hallmark difference between Piaget and Vygotsky relates specifically to the element of discovery. Both theorists identified the environment as significant for development; however, Piaget outlined self-initiated exploration and discovery, while Vygotsky highlighted the role of specific social interactions as a key factor in the development and learning processes. Vygotsky highlighted the social function and goal of communication as an essential aspect to consider in the collective study of thought and language. Vygotsky's work also emphasized the process of imaginative play to support the cognitive development of children. The act of play specifically aligns with the developmentally appropriate approach and importance of discovery and creativity necessary for learning during the early childhood years. The acts of drill work outside of a generalizable scenario may result in more difficulty for a child to retain and utilize new information, including word meaning, sentence structures, and social communication, across varied contexts and scenarios. Play provides a solid platform to create imaginative situations that introduce and build on real-life encounters allowing children to learn through engaging in the interactions with the environment. Consider a young child who plays grocery store with a group of friends at preschool. Perhaps the teacher has introduced several books specific to the grocery store, where the food is grown, the act of paying for food, and other associated vocabulary to build important background knowledge. The children are then introduced to an imaginative play area in the classroom built upon the new knowledge introduced. They are now able to utilize the new information through the intentionally provided imaginative play opportunity to interact within the grocery store scenario. Additionally, the child may engage with grocery store play at home, generalizing the new information in a new environment, and perhaps, eventually, will communicate information about the grocery store while visiting the actual store with the parent. Consider the generalization potential of this and similar opportunities provided in early childhood classroom settings. This scenario often happens with the young children we work with, right? They engage in imaginative play within the classroom or at home and begin to broaden the use of the new concepts and knowledge to new scenarios in the natural contexts of their lives. Let's extend this concept a step further because with this growing body of language knowledge, a young child learning to read and write may comprehend a short passage about going to the grocery store with dad or develop a written approximation of a grocery list, using pictures or words to support development of written expression. Vygotsky builds our awareness of the social aspects and interactions used for learning within our environments (Vygotsky, 1962). Let's consider a *Communication Connection* related to the impact of play-based learning within your classroom or home environments.

COMMUNICATION CONNECTION

Spend a few minutes identifying areas of your classroom that may support the introduction of contextual play, schemas, or topics. What materials are present? Do the topics and areas in your classroom change or remain the same over the course of weeks, months, or a school year? Why have you chosen these topics? Do any of your topics, play areas, or imaginative play scenarios relate specifically to a concept unique to the community the children in your classroom live in?

1. **Consider if you have introduced the vocabulary, background knowledge, and appropriate social interactions to consider prior to children interacting with the particular area in the classroom.**
   We shouldn't assume that all young children in our classroom have been introduced or engaged in the same or even similar scenarios. Topics familiar to one child may be completely unknown to another child. Introduction to vocabulary and background knowledge related to each individual topic or scenario builds a strong foundation for all children to interact, adapt, and modify schemas to navigate and expand their interactions and language.

2. **Do you model language for use within a specified topic or play scenario? Perhaps, you discuss how you would order at restaurant or what the nurse might say to a patient at the doctor's office.**
   Similar to the information provided in Question 1, we need to provide scaffolded information to children, in order to ensure they have the language knowledge they need to

successfully engage in growing interactions within varied scenarios. Modeling language provides a starting point the child can build upon. It offers them the opportunity to meaningfully engage with peers in communication with a starting point linked to success.

3. **What are ways you could enhance these interactions and scenarios to support ongoing oral language development, as well as literacy development, including reading and writing?**
Consider ways you can provide written text within various play opportunities. This may include menus for restaurants, check-in paperwork for doctor or vet areas, grocery lists for grocery stores, books for the "waiting areas" in various play areas in the classroom. Informal inclusion of these various items introducing children to the literacy within society helps them to identify the items as information tools, allows children to begin to navigate obtaining and providing information within a literacy-based society, and builds awareness and knowledge of print in fun and imaginative ways.

As we conclude this chapter focused on theoretical discussion, I want to revisit the importance of the theoretical constructs associated with language development, offered in this chapter, and the insight they offer into the nature and nurture aspects of the development of language meaning, structure, and use. This chapter provided only a brief overview for the purpose of developing context as we continue to discuss speech and language acquisition, development, and use with a focus on the early childhood years, specifically birth to eight years. Understanding theoretical constructs associated with speech and language development can support and enhance our goal of providing optimal activities, opportunities, and strategies to plant seeds and build supportive bridges for effective, functional communication for successful academic and social communicative intents. Consideration of these theoretical constructs and foundational components offers us information for effectively shaping the environment for appropriately scaffolded play and interactions to continue to build vocabulary knowledge, model language structures with increasing complexity, and engage in the functional use of language across a variety of contexts. As we shift away from the specific focus on these theorists and their associated theoretical constructs, we will use their shared knowledge, researched evidence, and contributions to support our work focused on building strong communication foundations and continued speech and language growth and development for our young children. As we transition to Chapter 4, we will shift our discussion back in the direction of the practical application of the research with the topics of the development of vocabulary knowledge and phonological awareness. The research to practice connection is important as we identify evidence-based practices for supporting young children in acquiring, developing, and using language skills within their daily lives. Consideration of these theories of innate language faculties and environmental stimuli offer us a stable platform to identify the importance of vocabulary knowledge, as well as the importance of phonological awareness as we consider effective ways to support a child's speech and language acquisition, development, and learning.

Bibliography

Brown, R. (1973). *A First Language: The Early Stages.* Cambridge, MA: Harvard University Press.
Chomsky, N. (1965). *Aspects of a Theory of Syntax.* Cambridge, MA: MIT Press.
Chomsky, N. (1993). *Lectures on Government and Binding: The Pisa lectures.* ProQuest Ebook Central https://ebookcentral.proquest.com
Furth, H. G., Piaget, J., & Catholic University of America Department of Psychology. (1969). *Piaget and Knowledge: Theoretical Foundations.* Englewood Cliffs, NJ: Prentice-Hall.

Piaget, J., & Claparède, E. (1959). *The language and thought of the child* (Third edition revised and enlarged, Ser. International library of psychology, philosophy and scientific method). New York, NY: Humanities Press.

Piaget, J., Chomsky, N., & Piattelli-Palmarini, M. (1980). *Language and learning: The debate between Jean Piaget and Noam Chomsky.* Cambridge, MA: Harvard University Press.

Vygotsky, L. S. (1962). *Thought and language.* (E. Hanfmann & G. Vakar, Eds.) (Ser. Studies in communication). Cambridge, MA: MIT Press.

4

Vocabulary Building and Phonological Awareness: The How and Why

Let's talk about literacy! Over the course of my career as a speech-language pathologist, my role in the support of literacy development has grown and evolved thanks to working alongside talented and knowledgeable teachers who have taught me so much about literacy, combined with the continued growth of the speech-language pathologist's role within the literacy framework as outlined in the Every Student Succeeds Act and ASHA's speech-language pathology scope of practice. Additionally, my continued study of the interface of language within the literacy framework, particularly when considering reading comprehension and written expression, has continued to solidify the importance of the speech-language pathologist's role in supporting the acquisition and development of language to positively impact and support literacy development, including reading and writing. Working collaboratively with early childhood educators has contributed to my knowledge of the foundational skills needed to build and support a young child's development of a strong literacy framework. A solid and strong literacy foundation is important for reading, writing, and spelling in school and in life. As mentioned in an earlier chapter, we know that we live in a literate society with an ongoing need to communicate, read, process, and understand written text. Consider all the ways you obtain and convey information through reading and writing on a daily basis. Do you read the newspaper or news stories on social media, use road signs, read a menu, or write a text or email? These are only a few examples of all the ways we communicate and gain an understanding of our world through various literate modes. Establishing these early literacy skills for effective expression and comprehension is an ongoing goal for parents and early childhood colleagues to build functional expression and understanding within our literate world. The purpose of this chapter is not to debate what factors contribute most significantly to the development of reading or which skills are most important or the most effective methods of reading instruction, but instead, will take a big picture approach to identifying both vocabulary and phonological awareness as important building blocks for the literacy learning process. The chapter will serve to outline specific terminology, supporting literature and research evidence, and examples of vocabulary and phonological awareness activities, accompanied by expected ages of various components associated with these developmental components when appropriate.

Consideration of emergent literacy may be helpful as we explore the continuum of literacy development. Teale and Sulzby (1986) define emergent literacy as the knowledge and skills prior to the development of reading and writing. It is important to consider that literacy development is ongoing, rather than a moment in time in which literacy is mastered. Literacy encompasses many skills and shouldn't be viewed as all or nothing. Children may vary in their development and mastery of various skills within the literacy framework. Emergent literacy highlights the importance of literacy exposure and interaction during the early childhood years, including the recognition that reading, writing, and oral language don't develop in isolation of each other. Additionally, consideration of the role the environment and associated experiences play in literacy development is a key component aligning to the goals of early childhood education, providing children opportunities to interact, learn, and grow within a play-based, language and literacy rich environment. For the purpose of our role in the literacy development of young children, combined with our strong understanding of the significant role that play has in the development of language, let's frame emergent literacy as the foundational blocks that children build upon for future reading, writing, spelling, and language. I believe we can incorporate this emergent literacy framework into intentional play-based scenarios within early childhood classroom and home interactions. We can incorporate explicit and implicit teaching opportunities within these intentional play-based learning opportunities.

Early childhood encompasses a significant and strategic introduction to literacy that continues to grow and develop beginning in the early childhood years, but continuing far beyond these early experiences. We engage in interactive book reading, shared dialogue using a wide variety of vocabulary and sentence structures, as well as play-based activities continuously building background knowledge and incorporating reading and writing introductions and practice opportunities. Incorporating these building block activities into daily experiences and real-life scenarios supports the generalization and retention of these skills for young children. I believe literacy is central to all of the early childhood interactions we encounter and shouldn't be a separate consideration. Literacy learning is and should be fun and a time of discovery and creativity for every young child. We need to keep in mind the importance of scaffolding these opportunities and working within the zone of proximal development based on the individual strengths and levels of performance of each child. Literacy learning, like all learning, is not a one size fits all approach or timeline. Interacting within our literate society opens up a whole new world of information for young children to explore through their play, social interactions, and authentic communication encounters! As we frame our literacy discussion, I want to pause to consider our next *Communication Connection*.

COMMUNICATION CONNECTION

Take time to look around and investigate your classroom or your home. Note toys, activities, classroom areas, or pretend play scenarios that support literacy development. Identify five of these that jump out at you immediately without giving it much thought. You may quickly identify more than five during your brief observation. Using the identified toys, activities, areas, or play scenarios as the guide for this reflection, let's reflect on literacy opportunities within your classroom or home with the following questions.

1. **List or discuss with colleagues the five activities, toys, classroom areas, or pretend play scenarios you identified.**
2. **What are the ways each supports beginning and ongoing literacy development?**
3. **Do these activities incorporate vocabulary development, phonological awareness, reading development with letter identification, books, interaction with written text or picture communication, opportunities for exploring written expression in any format, including pictures, letters, words, or a combination of these?**
4. **Consider ways you might enhance these opportunities by providing additional literacy components. For example, in the restaurant pretend play area, are there menus? Could the children create the menus with pictures or written words? In your block area, could you incorporate opportunities for children to conceptualize their building plans on "blueprints" talking about size, shape, and engaging in inquiry and problem-solving when the structure built is not foundationally strong and continues to topple over?**

    This could be a great way to incorporate the introduction of new descriptive words that will increase the complexity of oral language, but also build background knowledge for future reading comprehension and written expression. I find it beneficial in practice to pose questions, plant a few idea seeds, and then let children use and share their inner creativity, critical thinking, and problem-solving with peers and with me. I want to encourage independent thinking and determination when a challenge surfaces because these are opportunities to develop and practice important life skills, including persistence, problem-solving, and collaborative thinking. Think of the questions you offer and the supportive foundation you provide as the building blocks for current and future literacy learning that is necessary for reading, writing, and spelling. In some cases, there is a need to build bridges to guide or facilitate more complex language within a scenario. Reflect on ways you provide support and scaffold language form, content, and use during these interactions, along with, continuing to build independence.

Now that you have engaged in another opportunity for a reflective communication connection, let's look deeper into the specific and focused areas of vocabulary and phonological awareness development. We will explore the link to language, reading, writing, and spelling. Early childhood experiences have the potential to play a key role in developing a robust vocabulary foundation that will support future reading comprehension, written expression, oral expression, and reading comprehension. Notice I mentioned "play" again, because I believe the impact of play builds creativity, while supporting interactions with various schemas relevant to natural contexts within daily life. It is important to recognize the value of play and specifically the importance of child-directed play and learning. Providing young children with a framework with the space to think, problem-solve, ask questions, and interact with various scenarios supports the language learning process. Additionally, we will explore the impact of building strong phonological awareness skills to support continued literacy development.

Vocabulary

Words – the meaning of those words, words with multiple meanings, using words appropriately in a variety of contexts – all of these words we speak, read, and write are so much more than *just words*, right? Hart and Risley (2003) stated that stronger vocabulary during the early childhood years is linked to stronger reading outcomes. This research supports the view that building a robust and comprehensive vocabulary repertoire during the early childhood years is directly linked to reading outcomes. Many of you reading this book may be nodding your heads, "yes," because you see the reality of this research play out each day when you are working with and observing the language and literacy of the young children you know. You may be considering the impact of the strong vocabulary base for your kindergarten, 1st grade, or 2nd grade students who are engaged in the reading and writing learning journey. The challenging impact of a lacking vocabulary base may become more evident as a child is beginning to engage in more complex, decontextualized reading and writing activities. There are specific ways in which vocabulary is linked to reading outcomes, including improved reading comprehension and recognition of words during reading (National Early Literacy Panel, 2008). When we consider this information, it becomes abundantly clear why some of our students begin to experience frustration as they move forward with higher level reading and writing tasks. When early elementary school children inform me that they don't like books or reading or writing, I want to know more. I feel compelled to ask why, and often ask children to tell me more about their dislike of these activities. First, I want to understand from the child's perspective what they don't like. Honestly, in many, if not most cases, children can provide the most valuable information for determining ways to offer support and encouragement in the literacy arena because they are the only ones who truly can understand what they are experiencing. I want to know, what is it about books, reading, or writing that makes these nonpreferred activities for a child? Is it a lack of vocabulary or background knowledge, missing phonological awareness skills important for decoding, or difficulty organizing oral language into written expression for writing tasks? These are only a few of the questions that I ponder when I encounter a child who prefers not to engage in these literacy activities. Although a child may not have the ability to articulate specifically a lack of vocabulary or phonological awareness challenges, a child can tell us in his or her own words why something is difficult. I believe offering a child the opportunity to share in his or her own words provides affirmation to the child that his or her perspective matters.

I am a speech-language pathologist, so I believe for me, by the sheer nature of my career path, I enjoy words, reading, and writing. However, I also distinctly remember books being a significant part of my childhood beginning at a young age and continuing through my present daily life, including teaching my college students, researching and writing to learn and grow along my professional journey, engaging in literacy activities with my speech and language clients, and reading for pleasure when I find the time. In fact, many of my earliest memories include engaging in interactions with books, including reading with my parents and grandparents. I believe a few pictures may also exist of me enjoying a book during my early childhood years. I tend to think that my ongoing love of reading started in those early years thanks to my parents and continued to grow out of that early exposure to, and shared interaction with, books and written text. I still enjoy a good story and children's literature is still one of my favorite sections in the library. The imagination, the creativity, the stories, and lessons found within children's books offer ways to open a child's world of learning to new words, sentence structures, speech sounds, and social language. Books are often at the top of my gift-giving list for young children in my life. I use books often in my speech and language intervention sessions and I embrace opportunities to offer a literacy lesson to a classroom of young learners. I see these opportunities as ways of opening the world of meaning found in words to children within the context of daily experiences. Remember in Chapter 1 when I mentioned the importance of my focus on generalization of speech and language skills and knowledge into the daily contexts of a child's life?

Books are a wonderful way to incorporate literacy and learning into contextualized environments, as well as provide a foundation for discussion of vocabulary and background knowledge embedded in children's literature.

It is important as we consider vocabulary that we support the implementation and practice of teaching and learning of vocabulary in an evidence supported manner. I want to begin by discussing the cognitive processing approach to learning because it will help guide our understanding of one theoretical construct that may help with understanding the word learning process. This is not the only theoretical framework; however, it will be the focus of this vocabulary discussion. The cognitive processing approach focuses on active processing of the association between a word and referent (Akhtar, Jipson, & Callahan, 2001). Consideration of the cognitive processing approach combined with empirical scientific evidence provides important foundation information for supporting vocabulary development. First, children require the teaching of word definitions through explicit and implicit teaching opportunities to establish mental representations for word comprehension that are necessary for using words in similar or novel contexts (Beck & McKeown, 2007). Xuan and Dollaghan (2013) state that, for some languages, specified parts of speech may, in fact, be easier to learn than others. It is important to consider individual languages when determining which parts of speech may prove easier to learn in a specific language. In my practical experience, this may impact implicit compared to explicit vocabulary teaching. In many cases, in the scope of my clinical work, I see children actively process and store in their memory words used often or words with specific salient features they can relate to with their daily routines and activities. During language intervention, with a goal of increasing functional vocabulary, I will often begin working on nouns with a young child who has a primary language of English because they label specific, concrete objects. Nouns often provide opportunities for increased tangible learning opportunities, including seeing, hearing, tasting, and touching. These sensory experiences often build a stronger and faster link between the object's label and actual object because there is active processing of these associations using various modalities. Clay, Gill, Glynn, McNaughton, and Salmon (2007) identified the importance of the number of opportunities necessary for processing words and storing mental representations for future retrieval. Studies providing evidence of the need for multiple exposures for word learning are dependent upon the individual child, word learning environment, and the type of word being learned (Wasik, Hindman, & Snell, 2016). McGregor, Sheng, and Ball (2007) stated 40 exposures is the estimated number of interactions necessary to process and learn new words. Additional supporting evidence for word processing and learning provided by Clay et al. (2007) stated that up to 200 exposures may be necessary for processing and learning new words. When we consider this range in necessary exposures, spanning from 40 to potentially 200 exposures, evidence of the importance of frequent and meaningful exposure within the early childhood education environment, combined with the home environment, is evident in order to reach the optimal necessary exposures for establishing solid mental representations of the word labels to object referent associations. Additionally, children need opportunities to utilize novel vocabulary words as they are learning these additions to their vocabulary repertoire. These opportunities are practice for the child to use the word and obtain feedback from listeners related to the appropriateness of the word when used during daily interactions. Have you ever experienced a young child using a new word, but, perhaps, the word is not used with exact accuracy? Perhaps a word is used frequently by a young child when he or she is trying it out? An example that comes to mind includes a young child beginning to use the word "actually." The child may start each sentence with the new word. In some cases, the new word is utilized appropriately and, in other cases, it may be less accurate. An additional example is the word "because." In my experience, many children begin to demonstrate awareness of the cause and effect explanation purpose of "because" but may not use the word with mastery in all situations during the learning process. We may note how cute it is when a young child uses these new words, but when we pause to consider that they are actually engaging and interacting in the world around them to learn the appropriate context for the use of these words, it is an interesting example of the language-learning process.

As I have continued to review the literature and research studies, as well as implemented evidence-based practice when targeting literacy development in young children as a clinical practitioner, I have become more confident in my belief that early childhood education environments, including home environments, birth to kindergarten early childhood education settings, combined with the early elementary school years, are an optimal context for establishing and strengthening new word learning, including contextualized and decontextualized language. We will revisit language intervention within daily contexts and relevant to an individual child's life in a future chapter. I believe supporting children who need speech and language intervention in ways specifically and intentionally linked to the curriculum, combined with the context of daily environments, interactions, and routines, including the home and school environments, significantly serves the goal of generalizing functional and effective communication into a child's daily social interactions, learning activities, and routines.

It is important to visit contextualized and decontextualized vocabulary in this chapter because words vary in the frequency of use in specific contexts. Identification of Tier 1, Tier 2, and Tier 3 vocabulary seems appropriate at this stage of our vocabulary discussion. When we consider word learning, it will serve us well to understand the types of words that are learned easily during the context of daily routines and oral language without a need for explicit teaching, as well as those words that may require more explicit instruction to build awareness and comprehension for future use in oral language expression written expression, and reading comprehension.

In continuing the discussion of vocabulary and the acquisition and development of the core foundation necessary for future literacy activities, specifically reading and writing, it is important to identify the various vocabulary tiers and the relationship to the need for explicit teaching. When considering Tier 1 vocabulary, minimal explicit teaching is necessary because these words occur frequently across a variety of contexts within the context

TABLE 4.1
Tiered Vocabulary

Tier	Definition	Examples
1	Everyday words used often in conversational speech	walk, go, apple, cat
2	High frequency words occurring across content areas	complicated, verify, opposite, enormous
3	Domain specific words	predict, understand, explain, answer

Beck, McKeown, and Kucan (2013).

of oral language. Children are exposed to Tier 1 words in multiple interactions and communicative encounters from the early stages of speech and language development. Revisit the example of Tier 1 words offered in Table 4.1. In considering the use of Tier 1 words, it is easy to see how children are exposed to these words in a frequent and ongoing manner beginning in the early stages of language acquisition and development. Children often learn and begin to utilize Tier 1 vocabulary within daily interactions to request, deny, and comment. Tier 2 vocabulary offers a more complex vocabulary inventory, specifically words that may not appear as often within oral language but, instead, are found more frequently in written text. The lack of frequency in oral language makes it necessary to provide explicit instruction to introduce, teach, and solidify knowledge and use of these words in daily interactions. Introduction and discussion of Tier 2 words during the preschool and early elementary years is, once again, an opportunity to build the solid literacy foundation needed for future literacy learning success. Finally, Tier 3 words are found within specific content areas or are characterized as domain specific. We are all aware of the specific vocabulary within areas of scientific, mathematical, historical, or literature study, to name a few. These words are generally explicitly taught within the context of the specifically associated subject area. I want to offer an opportunity to engage in personal investigation or collegial discussion specific to vocabulary teaching and learning with our next *Communication Connection*.

COMMUNICATION CONNECTION

I am going to assume that your classroom includes a comprehensive collection of children's literature or you have easy access to a variety of wonderful children's literature to share with the children in your class. I am going to ask you to identify four or five of your favorite children's books individually or as a collective group of colleagues. It is highly likely you have read the books you have chosen to or with children more times than you can recall. Perhaps, you have them memorized or they are linked to a favorite theme you look forward to each school year. In fact, perhaps the books bring a sense of happiness or warm memories due to consistent excitement or positive responses from children each time you introduce the book(s). I am going to ask you to build on the exciting thoughts, combined with the literacy building block of vocabulary, and identify vocabulary learning opportunities.

1. Identify various Tier 1 words within the book. As you engage in purposeful identification of Tier 1 words in the text, what becomes evident to you? Do you notice words that are used frequently in daily interactions in natural contexts, including your classroom and associated school activities, as well as home environments? Is there context supporting the vocabulary knowledge associated with these words? Note how often you feel the need to explicitly teach these words, outside of play-based or interactive opportunities that occur often within the natural environment.
2. Let's now move our identification and discussion to Tier 2 words within the book. Identify two to four Tier 2 words within the same book. As you begin to identify these vocabulary words, does anything different become evident to you? Are these words found with the same level of contextualized support? Do these words require explicit teaching and more focused

dialogue? Note how often you are explicitly teaching these words during shared book reading activities. Are there ways you could identify these words and begin to incorporate increased explicit teaching into shared book reading opportunities with students individually or collectively within large group learning situations? Consider the potentially positive impact the explicit exposure and intentional discussion during the early childhood years may have on future reading comprehension and written expression tasks.
3. Does the book include Tier 3 vocabulary words? Is the book domain or content specific? Consider incorporating Tier 3 words into domain-specific activities. For example, a science experiment in your classroom could involve the discussion of a "hypothesis" or a "prediction" of what the students think will happen.

We have valuable opportunities to build intentional literacy-supporting activities into daily interactions during the early childhood years, but we should also identify the strategies, problem-solving, and critical-thinking foundation we can instill in our young learners. Verbally processing through the steps to problem-solve and critically think may provide young learners the opportunity to learn and practice these steps that will support future navigation of literacy tasks of increased complexity. When we read for the purpose of gaining information, it isn't necessary to look up each word we read or even each word we don't know the meaning of as we read. Why? We are able to use context to problem-solve and critically think to determine the meaning of the text we are reading. I believe there is value in beginning to build this thought process and supportive problem-solving into the early childhood dialogue. The reality is that many interactions socially and academically with oral, reading, and written language will appear in a narrative format initially; however, as children continue to progress into higher academic levels, entering the middle and secondary school years, learning often includes increased interactions with expository text. Expository text often includes decontextualized vocabulary and the expectation for independent completion of tasks and learning grows. The vocabulary thinking, learning, and problem-solving started in the early childhood years can build a supportive structure for a student to navigate these higher-level, more complex learning scenarios. Consider this potential impact as you are sharing, teaching, and reinforcing the acquisition, development, and growth of a strong vocabulary foundation for all the young language learners in your life.

Phonological Awareness

As a speech-language pathologist, I have chosen to make phonological awareness a significant target of my work to support reading and spelling success. Phonological awareness is the umbrella term that includes the ability to identify and manipulate speech sound units. Phonemic awareness, specifically sound awareness, falls under the umbrella of phonological awareness. A focus on phonological awareness during the early childhood years builds the foundation for the ability to decode words, a skill necessary for reading and spelling. In Chapter 2, we talked about phonemes, the smallest units of sound. If you recall, these small units of sound do not have meaning; however, when we combine these individual phonemes into meaningful units, we use these meaningful words for effective communication. Explicit teaching of phonological awareness, including phonemic awareness, during the early childhood years serves to support the development and progression of reading, writing, and spelling skills.

As we begin to explore the development of phonological awareness skills, it is important to make the true connection between the impact of exposure during the early childhood years and future literacy development, including reading, writing, and spelling. Bryant et al. (1989) stated phonological awareness skill development has a role in the prediction of future reading ability. These emergent phonological awareness skills are developed during the early childhood years, thus potentially connecting reading skill acquisition to the relevant phonological awareness activities embedded in early childhood environments. Rhyming is generally the first phonological awareness skill to emerge during the early childhood years. Young children begin to engage in rhyming games involving exploration of the concept of rhyming at approximately three years old. Children progress to the next level of rhyming abilities, including recognition of words that rhyme, at approximately four years of age. Finally, children are generally able to independently generate rhyming words in kindergarten. It is important to continue to recognize the individuality and range of speech and language developmental norms in determining if a young child is meeting these expected levels of skill developmental on an appropriate trajectory.

Given the supporting research evidence of the connection of phonological awareness to future reading ability, it is beneficial to continue to monitor the development of phonological awareness skills providing evidence of acquisition of foundational literacy skills. I am certain many, if not all, early childhood educators support the development of rhyming and accompanying phonological awareness skill development focused on building awareness of sounds, as well as the manipulation of sounds in words. Phonological awareness skill development encompasses identification of sounds in the initial or final position of words, phonemic blending, and phoneme deletion, to name a few of the skills. The listed phonological awareness tasks are simply a glimpse into a few of the ways I work on manipulating speech sounds with language learners. I always make these activities into fun games or play-based activities during the early years to make phonological awareness a fun introduction to future reading and writing development.

The ability to manipulate sounds has the potential to support the decoding of words for acquisition of fluent reading skills. Reading fluency without interruptions and disruptions in the reading process can positively impact a reader's ability to comprehend the text. Consider if you needed to decode each word or even several words when reading a text. The disruption in the reading fluency may likely impact your ability to understand

TABLE 4.2
Phonological Awareness Skills and Activities

Phonological Awareness Skill	Statement	Answer and Considerations
Sound Identification	I want you to tell me what sound is at the beginning of the word I say. What is the first or beginning sound in the word "sun".	/s/ Ensure the child understands the various positions in a word, including the understanding of the concepts "first" or "beginning".
Phoneme Blending	I am going to say some sounds and I want you to blend or put them together. What word do the sounds make? /k/ /æ/ /t/	"cat" Ensure the child understands the concept of blending or putting sounds together.
Phoneme Deletion	I am going to say a word and I want you to tell me what word is left if you delete or remove the /k/. What word is left if you remove the /k/ in the word /kæt/?	"at" Ensure the child understands the concept of deleting or removing sounds.

what you are reading. Table 4.2 outlines ways I have introduced these various activities to children and incorporated subsequent and ongoing opportunities to develop and practice these important phonological awareness skills. This is not meant to be an exhaustive list of phonological awareness activities but, instead, a glimpse into ways to introduce, engage in explicit teaching dialogue, and promote opportunities for practice to build a solid foundation to support future reading, writing, and spelling.

Scarborough (1990) identified significant relationships between children exhibiting reading problems in Grade 2 when compared to the same children's syntactic structure and phonological expression at the age of two and one-half years of age. This research supports the continued evidence that the impact of speech and language learning opportunities, teaching, and practice during the early childhood years is important to the future literacy success linked to reading literacy. This particular research points to syntax and phonology as key indicators to the potential for future reading challenges. Additionally, Bryant, Bradley, Maclean, and Crossland (1989) linked a significant connection specific to nursery rhyme knowledge at age three years of age, phonological awareness during the early childhood education years, and a child's success during the learning to read process. As mentioned earlier in this chapter, my purpose is not to debate specific approaches to reading instruction or the specific levels of importance of the related skills. Instead, my goal is to spark reflective thinking and consideration of the components connected to successful literacy development to support future reading, writing, and spelling. Additionally, I hope to ignite the consideration of increased focus on creative and fun phonological awareness activities to support a child's development of awareness, identification, and manipulation of language units and phonemes to support ongoing literacy development beginning in the early childhood years but continuing into later reading and writing development.

As a speech-language pathology practitioner, I believe that both vocabulary knowledge, as well as the ability to utilize context to problem-solve and critically think, combined with awareness and the ability to manipulate speech sounds and language units support reading fluency, reading comprehension, formulation of written expression, and accurate spelling, are necessary for successful progression of literacy learning. As a result, when I am invited to collaborate with a team to problem-solve ways to support a struggling reader, I will continue to ask questions about the depth and breadth of the student's vocabulary knowledge, as well as the student's phonological awareness skills, specifically the identification and manipulation of individual speech sounds. I would encourage you to reflectively consider these skills also in relationship to opportunities for practice and the potential impact of gaps in these skills when working with a child experiencing reading or writing challenges. As we continue our discussion with a transition to Chapter 5, we will begin to explore ways to establish and support an optimal communication environment for each and every child in your classroom.

Bibliography

Akhtar, N., Jipson, J., & Callahan, M. A. (2001). Learning words through overhearing. *Child Development*, 72(2), 416–430.

Beck, I. L., & McKeown, M. G. (2007). Increasing young low-income children's oral vocabulary repertoires through rich and focused instruction. *The Elementary Journal*, 107(3), 251–271.

Beck, I. L., McKeown, M. G., and Kucan, L. (2013). *Bringing Words to Life, Second Edition: Robust Vocabulary Instruction*. New York, NY: Guildford Press.

Bryant, P. E., Bradley, L., Maclean, M., & Crossland, J. (1989). Nursery rhymes, phonological skills, and reading. *Journal of Child Language*, 16, 407–428.

Clay, M., Gill, M., Glynn, T., McNaughton, T., & Salmon, K. (2007). *Record of oral language: Observing changes in the acquisition of language structures* (3rd ed.). New Zealand: Heineman.

Hart, B., & Risley, T. R. (2003). The early catastrophe: The 30 million word gap by age 3. *American Educator*, 27(1), 4–9.

McGregor, K. K., Sheng, L., & Ball, T. (2007). Complexities of expressive word learning over time. *Language, Speech, and Hearing Services in Schools*, 38(4), 353–364.

National Early Literacy Panel. (2008). *Developing early Literacy: Report of the National Early Literacy Panel*. Washington, DC: National Institute for Literacy.

Scarborough, H. S. (1990). Very early language deficits in dyslexic children. *Child Development*, 61, 1728–1743.

Teale, W. H. & Sulzby, E. (Eds.). (1986). *Emergent Literacy: Writing and Reading*. Norwood, NJ: Ablex.

Wasik, B. A., Hindman, A. H., & Snell, E. K. (2016). Book reading and vocabulary development: A systematic review. *Early Childhood Quarterly*, 37, 39–57.

Xuan, L. & Dollaghan, C. (2013). Language specific noun bias: Evidence from bilingual children. *Journal of Child Language*, 40, 1057–1075.

5

Building the Optimal Communication Environment for all Communicators

I have always enjoyed the excitement, curiosity, joy of learning through play, and creativity found within early childhood classrooms. The inquiry and ongoing opportunities for learning through interaction in the natural environment is at the heart of my goal as a speech-language pathologist to support children in the acquisition, development, and use of effective and functional speech and language skills within their individual natural contexts. During my years of clinical practice, this goal has aligned well with the focus of learning found within early childhood classrooms. Additionally, my time spent working in early elementary classroom environments has afforded me a wonderful opportunity to observe and participate in the continued growth of speech and language skills and the expansion of this knowledge and skills foundation into the areas of written expression and reading comprehension. There is generally never a boring moment in these natural settings and the minds of young children never seem to pause, but if we are able to allow ourselves a moment to observe, listen, and reflect, we gain significant and valuable insight into each individual child's most effective learning style and areas of interest to support contextualized language use and learning opportunities. This reality makes building effective modes of communication and supporting young children within the natural environment, through the development of optimal communication modalities for all children, a very important, complex, and, at times, challenging task. Providing ongoing opportunities for practicing communication within the safe and secure early education environments of home and school is an important component of the development of speech and language during the critical birth to eight years developmental timeframe.

In the previous chapters, we have built the foundation for the understanding of the acquisition and development of speech and language, including milestones, developmental trajectories, and theoretical constructs supporting the discussion surrounding speech and language acquisition and development. Additionally, the information in the previous chapters has offered us an important springboard for continuing our discussion with a focus on the importance of identifying, developing, and sustaining an optimal communication environment for all our young learners and communicators. Building upon a collective agreement that we want optimal communication for all children in our classrooms and homes, we can begin to consider how we will engage in action steps to create an environment that provides ongoing opportunities for effective and functional communication. It is important to maintain awareness that communication takes many forms and individual communication may vary among young children. Recognizing and utilizing each child's speech and language strengths to continue to build speech, language, and literacy skills is an effective start to building a comprehensive communication environment. I want to emphasize, once again, the importance of determining an individual child's strengths to build language and continue supporting the areas of difficulty. If we fail to note strengths with a focus on utilizing these to support language development and use, we are missing an important component of the child's communication profile. It is also important to revisit the importance of both nonverbal and verbal aspects of communication. Often, what a young child doesn't say may communicate more to us than the words they have spoken, or those words they are unable to speak. We must also maintain awareness that no assumption can be made about a child's ability to comprehend comprehensive and complex communication simply because the child is quiet or, alternatively, has reduced verbal expression. We shouldn't assume a child isn't able to understand, but we must also realize that we aren't able to assume the child is able to understand either. It is important to recognize that this consideration is two-fold. In some cases, children with deficits in the area of auditory comprehension or language understanding may retreat or shutdown during communication involving increased complexity. These instances may relate to multi-step directions, novel directions not linked to routines, or more complex, abstract vocabulary. Alternatively, we should not assume children who have reduced verbal expression are unable to comprehend complex language based on their lack of response. I also want to pause to recognize the importance of refraining from making assumptions related to language knowledge or comprehension based on a child's co-occurring areas of deficit, including the motor and sensory areas. This is an excellent time to revisit the importance of identifying each individual child's strengths and areas needing support. These multiple and individualized situations can be challenging to analyze, but it is important to support each child based on individual communication strengths and needs. Keep in mind that even our young communicators who are progressing along the typical speech and language trajectories and meeting milestones during the expected timeframe will also need continued support to promote their continued speech and language acquisition and development. Scaffolded speech and language learning will take root during these developmental opportunities as we work collaboratively to support children with diverse and individualized speech and language learning needs.

Identifying the need to reach and include all children specific to their individual communication strengths and needs requires us to focus on building a dynamic, interactive, and scaffolded communication environment. I recognize and understand that this is not an easy task and requires a significant amount of planning, thinking, responding in the moment, and engaging in reflective practices when there are communication breakdowns. A focus on identifying each individual child's strengths and communication deficits guides us in designing appropriate supports for increasing effective communication for all our young communicators. The exciting part for me in working in the area of birth to eight years is that early childhood educators understand, with an ongoing level of commitment and willingness to professionally grow, that developing an interactive, language rich environment positively impacts a young child's development far beyond what will be realized during the early childhood education and early elementary years. The speech and language seeds you plant during a child's early learning years continue to grow and have a positive impact as a child continues on the learning journey.

Where should we start in our identification, development, and implementation of an optimal communication environment? Understanding the environment is often the first step in determining how to interact within and engage in a specified setting, environment, or scenario. Consider times when you have visited a new environment or find yourself within a novel situation. Often, we may take time to begin to understand the environmental structure, routines, and procedures to ensure we are able to actively and successfully participate and interact within the setting. Although some school and home settings may have some level of similarity, it is often reasonable to identify that routines, procedures, interactions, materials, and expectations may vary to differing degrees across environments.

Given the need for me to build an understanding of any new early childhood environment I visit, I always begin with classroom or home observations to observe the items present, the routines associated with the setting, environmental characteristics, such as noise level, visual learning tools present, and the types of social and language interactions that are occurring.

For example, what are the typical routines within an individual classroom or home environment? Are these routines and procedures consistent? Are these explicitly taught? In addition to understanding similar and different components across various classroom environments, we must also consider how the home and school environments may also offer similarities and differences. Although there may be similarities spanning across the school and home settings, we should consider the variations that may be relevant. These differences across various environments and scenarios may result in a lack of environmental understanding necessary for effective communication as children move across various contexts as part of their daily life and routines. We should also consider that some children may be transitioning across many environments during a day, week, or month dependent upon individual child and family needs. In some cases, understanding the transitions an individual child makes across various environments can guide us in our understanding of communication modalities, interactions, and reactions to various situations. Teachers, parents, and early childhood colleagues will likely have many consistencies and similarities in their approach to the world of early childhood education and their interactions with young children; however, just as the children we work with have individual preferences, strengths, and approaches, we are all individuals also. The expected outcomes and developmental trajectory of the early childhood years follows a specified path, but there are many different ways to incorporate effective and necessary teaching and learning opportunities across various natural contexts. The primary focus of my goal to support optimal communication is to ensure communication attempts are effective and functional across a child's natural contexts. I highlight this same goal regardless of the area of language focus, including expressive, receptive, and social communication. The skills and abilities need to be generalized into daily environments and routines, as well as across a child's life contexts or environments to provide the young communicator with the skills necessary to successfully interact in the world. Let's consider this concept with an example found in our next *Communication Connection*.

COMMUNICATION CONNECTION

Consider a young preschooler who just turned three years old beginning her first year in school. She is joining your class three days each week. The young girl is happy, excited to begin school, and communicates effectively at home without any incident, based on parent report. She enjoys playing with her neighborhood friends, who are same-aged peers, outdoors. Her parents have no concerns about her development or communication. She is effectively communicating her wants and needs at home, as well as understanding what is said to her, including answering basic developmentally appropriate questions and following developmentally appropriate directions both within and outside of her routine. The young girl comes for an initial visit to your classroom and as expected she is excited but quiet since it is her first time in school. You interact with her parents and it is very apparent that they are very active and engaged in her learning and development. They share wonderful information about their young child, and it is clear they are excited but nervous about her beginning the school experience. You assure them she will have a wonderful time with opportunities to learn through play and interact with new friends.

The young girl comes to your class for her first day of school the next week. She separates from her parent without difficulty and almost immediately begins to play with her classroom peers. As the day progresses, she begins to attempt to verbally communicate with her peers and with you to request, comment, and share ideas, but you notice there are some communication breakdowns because her speech appears difficult to understand at times. She attempts to use some gestures she uses at home to communicate with you in the classroom with inconsistent success because you and the same-aged peers aren't familiar with her gesture communication system because she is new to the class. You notice by the end of the second week, she is experiencing more communication breakdowns and has started to abandon her attempts to communicate when there is a breakdown. She is not acting out with undesired behaviors; however, she is beginning to become quieter and is demonstrating reluctance to verbally express. When she does make attempts to communicate, she is now using mostly pointing or taking your hand to walk you over to what she is requesting. You recognize this significant change in her willingness to verbally communicate, as well as her growing retreat from interactions involving verbal expression.

1. **Have you ever experienced a similar situation with a young child who is a student in your classroom? Perhaps, the situation unfolded at a different rate, either slower or faster? What was your response to support the young child's functional and effective communication within the classroom environment?**
   This is not an uncommon scenario during the early childhood years. It is possible that a child has a highly effective communication method and mode at home with individuals who are familiar with the gestures the young child consistently uses and within the known context in a familiar environment, such as the home setting. Parents have an exceptional ability to anticipate and meet their child's needs, as well as learn the communication system of their child. I will continue to highlight the parent(s) as a child's first teacher, as well as the most valuable member of the child's team when considering speech and language assessment and intervention. Parents, guardians, and primary caregivers offer us important insight into ensuring that we understand a young child's communication profile.

   When the young child I write about above entered the school environment, she walked into a new environment with new contextual factors, including new routines, procedures, and expectations. She is now being asked to communicate with new communication partners, adults, and children, who may not have a solid grasp on her various communication methods, modes, strategies, and tools.

She is utilizing communication modalities that have been effective previously in her home environment but now is meeting the challenge of decreased effectiveness. In many situations, this can result in unanticipated communication breakdowns. Consider how you might work in partnership with the parent to support this young child in her new environment. I will offer some ideas, but this is not an exhaustive list of strategies to consider.

   a. Discuss with the young child's parents the gestures, pointing, or other methods the child uses to communicate in the home environment. Talk about ways to utilize and generalize those methods into the new early childhood environment. This will accomplish several supportive outcomes, including parent–teacher partnership, building skills across various contexts and environments, and demonstrating to the child and family the desire to empower this young child to use the skills that offer her a platform for effective and functional communication. Developing a consistent communication system spanning both the home and school contexts will support increased communication confidence for the young child. Even when a child experiences decreased speech clarity due to speech sound errors, we want to consider ways that we can continue to build and develop receptive and expressive language skills. We want to ensure that speech sound errors don't slow the progress of language skills.

   b. Consider ways to offer additional communication bridges to support this young child as she builds her communication abilities and confidence in a new environment. In addition to providing communication bridges, can you plant seeds for continued speech sound and language acquisition and development? You could ask the young child, "Could you show me?" or "Can you tell me in a different way?" when a communication breakdown occurs. It is valuable to demonstrate patience and give full attention to the child during her attempt to utilize the communication support. This will allow her an opportunity to use an alternative method to convey a thought, share an idea, or request. Consider providing a model of the effective and functional use of these skills in your daily classroom communication. Perhaps, you might verbally express an idea and then utilize pointing, simple gestures, or signs to identify and model alternate and supportive ways to communicate information.

c. Provide information specific to the strategies you are using in her new early childhood environment to her parents. Ask for their feedback and identify if any of the new communication bridges in the classroom environment could be used and practiced within the home environment. Keep in mind that most often a child may feel more confident and secure in a known environment, when compared to a novel setting. Eventually, the early childhood environment will become a known environment with familiar listeners and known contexts, but during the initial transition the child will need time to acclimate to these various components within the new context.

d. Finally, this example does not provide enough information to determine if a speech screening or assessment would be warranted, so we will not address this discussion during this *Communication Connection*. We will talk in more detail about speech and language screening and assessment referrals, as well as need for intervention, in Chapter 6; however, in some instances, this may be an appropriate time to explore a referral for a speech screening or assessment with the child's parent. In some cases, children will benefit from classroom supports, but there are times when a speech and/or language assessment, to determine the need for specifically and individually designed intervention to target speech and language deficits, is necessary and appropriate.

The *Communication Connection* dialogue outlined above provides one example of a situation that may occur in the early childhood classroom environment. The situation highlights the way we need to consider various situations, known and unknown communication strategies and tools, the context of the home and school environments, and individual child and family strengths and challenges to build a supportive and effective communication environment for young children. Identifying the components of the transition from the home environment to the education environment is a key factor as we consider the speech and language acquisition and development process, as well as the generalization of effective and functional communication across all natural environments and contexts. Let's consider another situation that I have experienced many times in clinical practice involving the transitions young children experience. If a young child completed preschool, kindergarten, or 1st grade within a highly structured classroom environment with an explicitly taught, specified, and known routine, supported with visual cues, verbal direction repetition, and multiple reminders, and the child now moves into the next grade with a focus on instruction that is primarily verbal directions without visual cues, combined with routines that vary each day, this has the potential to impact a young communicator's ability to effectively process and comprehend information or clearly express ideas. Again, we need to revisit the idea that when we enter a new environment, we also may need time to understand the routines, procedures, and expectations. These transitions are part of the reality of our lives. They are also important for a child to begin to learn to adapt and navigate various situations. Although these transitions provide opportunities for generalization, we need to be cautious that we recognize the complexity of these transitions. We need to work to identify what makes an optimal communication environment for an individual child and determine ways to ensure the child continues to have access to the strategies and tools for effective and functional communication when these transitions occur. It is important to note that children grow in their skills and knowledge, so it is possible that the tools and strategies that are necessary for an optimal communication environment during preschool may differ from those needed for optimal communication in kindergarten. It is also possible that the basis of a strategy or tool will remain the same, but the presentation will be adapted. For example, a visual schedule may begin as pictures, transition to words and pictures, then to words alone, and then potentially to a calendar. The adaptations grow with the child and promote organization and independence as a young child progresses through school building functional tools for successful language expression and understanding.

As we move into a deeper discussion of ways to provide optimal communication opportunities, I want to pause to reflect on the overall goal we want to achieve alongside our young communicators. I always focus on a goal of supporting the development of communication skills, while promoting the individual child's independence to the greatest extent possible, based on the individual child's strengths and needs. To the greatest extent possible, I work to provide children with the supportive tools they need to independently navigate a particular environment with the hope that strategies can generalize to other scenarios and settings. Remember, even children following a typical trajectory for speech and language development are likely to experience communication breakdowns. We all experience communication breakdowns at times. Providing an optimal communication environment isn't simply for children in need of speech or language intervention. We can identify strategies and tools to support all young communicators, particularly during speech and language acquisition and development.

In the following section, I have outlined several strategies and tools that I have used in my clinical practice, along with collaborative parents and educators, to support the success of young children in successfully navigating and interacting within classrooms and homes. This outline is not meant to be exhaustive in nature. There isn't a way to list every beneficial strategy and tool for each child because children are individual and much of our job is determining which strategies and tools are most effective for each child. I have listed a few key ideas that I have found beneficial across many of the classrooms and homes I have been afforded the opportunity to participate and collaborate in to support young children's speech and language learning. These tools and strategies have the potential to support all young communicators, regardless of the need for speech and language assessment and intervention, as they travel on their communication and learning journey. They are simply ways to build a communication friendly environment for all, in support of speech and language acquisition and development, as well as positive social interactions.

Schedules

In fact, classroom tools and strategies can support all young learners, while being individualized as needed for students in need of additional supports. I am going to begin our discussion with the identification of schedules as a beneficial and, in my opinion, necessary tool for any classroom. Additionally, in many cases, I would also recommend a home schedule. I strongly support the use of schedules, in classrooms and homes. Why do I love schedules so much? Let me pose this scenario for you to consider. You have arrived at your classroom for the day and realize you left your phone at home. Your phone has your schedule for the day, and it is the only place you have recorded your daily schedule. You vaguely remember you have an appointment in the afternoon, but can't remember the time. You also remember you are supposed to contact a colleague in the morning, but the contact information is in your phone. You don't have the series of events for the day committed to memory so you are unable to determine what the event sequence is or what will come next in your day. Have any of you ever experienced a similar scenario? How did this sequence of events make you feel? What emotions did you experience? Perhaps frustration, anxiety, or fear of missing something important are only a few that may have crossed your mind. As you read this scenario, did you begin to experience some of these reactions even though this is a hypothetical? Did you vividly recall a day when something similar happened? Let's continue this discussion by reframing this situation for a young child's experience with similar scenarios occurring in classrooms. The child attends school and knows the general routine, but today it is raining so there won't be any outside time and it is difficult to remember if lunch occurs before or after large group reading time. Could the child experience some of the same emotions you may have identified? Could the child be confused and concerned about not knowing the sequence of events? Could the child's inability to identify what is expected next cause frustration or anxiety? I think there is definitely the potential for any combination of these feelings and reactions. In considering this, let's add in that the child experiencing these emotions may be unable to effectively express how the lack of a schedule to reference the daily events impacts her understanding. Let's consider that a similar scenario may result in feelings of disorganization or uncertainty. I want to reiterate that even a child with speech and language skills that result in expected milestones and follow the typical developmental trajectory may experience these emotions and reactions. Many of us prefer to know what to expect during our daily routines and we prefer to know when those routines will deviate from the plan, as well as the new expectations. Personally, I know that I prefer to know what is expected and when plans may change. It offers me a sense of security and understanding. I think it is highly likely that some of the young children in our classrooms may desire the same during their daily activities.

In addition to providing children with a plan for the day and predicting expected events and activities, schedules have additional benefits. In my opinion, schedules have the ability to support and build independence, as well as enhance the development of organizational skills in young children. If a young child has a schedule to reference, independently determining the routine as well as processing changes in the routine are feasible options. Additionally, we are modeling for a young child the way to organize a day into distinct, concrete, activities, or events to ensure tasks are accomplished, the appropriate sequence is followed, and adaptations or modifications are accounted for when planning. We provide a landscape and then we demonstrate how the plan can be modified and adapted. It is how life works, right?

We develop a plan for our day and then we adapt as new information or changes are necessary.

Schedules can take many forms and can be easily modified and adapted based on individual and collective classroom or home needs. I am going to offer several suggestions for schedules I have utilized or provided to families for home use in the past. It is important to note that each child, family, and classroom may demonstrate different needs, so we need to consider the most effective schedule modality in each situation. Visual schedules provide pictures to support a child in understanding and processing the sequence of events and activities of a given day. Visual schedules generally involve pictures specific to the activities and events. The type of pictures can vary, including actual photographs of real objects or people, drawings created by early childhood educators or parents, or other pictures obtained by the educator or parent. As a simple reminder, please ensure you pay attention to copyright of images you find and use to determine if it is appropriate to utilize the picture(s) that you have selected based on the intended use policies. Additionally, in relationship to visual schedules, consider a young child who may process information most effectively by experiencing real objects through touch. In this case, I have used real objects attached to the schedule pictures to allow a child to touch and experience the object for each activity included in the daily or activity schedule. For example, I have used a small book attached to the schedule picture for large group circle time because a book was a hallmark representation for the circle time activities and for the individual child. In this case, the visual picture included a picture of a book, a real object book, and the word "book." The schedule including these various levels of representation allowed for scaffolding to meet the needs of young children at a variety of communication levels. A schedule structured in this way supported the children who benefited from tactile and visual input, those responding well to a picture representation of a book, and the young learners who were beginning to explore written text as part of their communication system. This schedule met the comprehension goals of children with needs spanning various communication tools and strategies by using a scaffolded approach.

Visual Supports

I want to continue our discussion of visuals because they are extremely important in many cases to support the comprehension or understanding of language during communication. Visual representations of emotions, as well as the directions given in various settings, offer significant support during language development. Visuals aligned with the presented auditory information provide an additional mode of information presentation and offer a supportive tool for young children experiencing difficulty with comprehension and processing of auditory information. Additionally, visuals offer increased exposure to a variety of words, which provides support for expressive language and the potential development of mental representations of vocabulary. Think of visuals as clues in the environment to assist children with processing and understanding information in combination with auditory information. Visuals aren't required to be in the form of pictures. In fact, many times, we use nonverbal communication, in combination with verbal communication, to support a child with following routines or participating in various activities. Gestures, familiar signs, and pointing are a few of the nonverbal communication examples we may use to support young learners. The use of visuals can expand beyond communication interactions and routines. Consider how labeling toy shelves or storage containers supports building language expression, comprehension, categorization, and organization. Children can match toys to the appropriate storage container and then match the container to the shelf, with increasing independence. Children can begin to identify similarities and differences among toys, moving from identification that is specific to the actual, tangible object to noting these descriptive characteristics in pictures.

Additionally, consider how you may provide visuals to identify various areas of the classroom. Do you utilize words, pictures, real objects to label specific activities or classroom areas? Are they easy to identify for the children in the classroom? Are these visual representations at eye level for children to see and identify? Use of visuals to differentiate areas of the classroom can provide concrete evidence for children about what toys will be found in the various areas, as well as encourage specific play-based scenarios to promote language and social interactions, based on the expected activities associated with a specified area. I believe the more we can provide young children with the visual, verbal, and nonverbal communication tools needed to navigate their environment, the more likely they are to engage in interactions and play-based learning.

Building Background Knowledge

It benefits all children to have a grasp on the vocabulary and knowledge associated with a variety of topics, play areas or scenarios, or activities prior to engaging with that specific entity. It is much easier for a child to actively participate in the learning process when the child is provided with general information, including vocabulary, examples of ways to interact in a given scenario, and components necessary for successful engagement. I want to provide a couple of examples for you to consider in order to provide insight into ways this may *play* out within classrooms. In this first scenario, I want you to consider the introduction of a bakery playset into your classroom. The set is complete with a baker's hat, pans, a recipe book, several representations of baked goods, a cash register, and bakery boxes. Perhaps some young learners in your classroom have eaten cookies and have enjoyed a yummy piece of cake, but have never been to a bakery or helped with the actual baking process. We provide children significant support for engaging in meaningful interactions to practice and develop language and social skills when we offer the opportunity to build background knowledge. This could include reading books about bakeries and baking, highlighting important related vocabulary, talking about the various roles of individuals in the bakery setting, and encouraging children to share ideas about ways to play in the bakery area. In this case, we have provided a foundation for success and empowered children to use the background knowledge that they hold in order to interact with the specific context and make adaptations, as well as expand the bakery concept within play-based interaction. The second example I will provide takes into consideration a writing task. Let's consider a task involving children beginning to explore written expression combining pictures and written words. You ask the children to share information about their favorite summer activity. Independently, children will provide information, but let's think about ways we can continue to build background and vocabulary knowledge in order to support both the semantic content (vocabulary) and syntactic structure (sentence and word constructions) of language. What if, prior to this activity, you modeled your description of your favorite activity, including descriptive words? Often, children will provide a concrete description, but need prompts to consider descriptive words. If they identify the park, what do they specifically like about the park? Is it going **fast** down the **big** slide? Is it digging in the **wet** sand in the sandbox? We begin to model ways to incorporate descriptive words that are important in written expression. Often, children may include these words in oral expression, but let's assist them in incorporating them into written expression. Written expression is a complex language form. Support for developing a strong foundation of descriptive words can provide a valuable contribution to future development of written expression. The impact of this language development is important in the early education years, but consider how the importance will continue to grow as they are asked to write essays for different purposes, or they are asked to give oral presentations with description to support a researched topic. This is another example of the way in which the important language form, content, and use modalities develop a foundation during the early childhood education years that will continue to grow and develop far exceeding the child's early years.

As you consider how to provide an optimal communication environment for young children, I encourage you to identify and utilize the strategies and tools outlined that will provide benefit to your classroom. I would encourage you to spend time considering the following questions that I am providing in the summary to this chapter. They are meant to offer additional reflective opportunities for individuals or a collective group to consider current practices and potential ways to enhance optimal communication opportunities within the classroom setting, recognizing the importance of language expression and comprehension, social language use, and speech clarity in the successful use of effective communication.

1. Are there ways to increase clarification or explicitly teach and represent expectations, routines, and procedures within your classroom? For young children experiencing difficulty with understanding these classroom components, how might you develop strategies or tools to support understanding through use of their individual strengths?
2. Do children in your classroom have a clear understanding of the daily activities and events? How do you represent inevitable changes to this standard schedule because we know things happen to alter our best plans? Do you utilize a whole class schedule? Would individual schedules support the learning and development of any children in your classroom? Are there specific tasks that require individual activity schedules to support the development of independence as a young child navigates successful completion of the task? If your classroom doesn't currently include the use of a schedule, are there ways to incorporate one? Would it be beneficial to provide additional visual pictures or written words for the child to reference for clarification?
3. How do you support children who experience a communication breakdown resulting from reduced speech clarity? Do you offer opportunities to "show you" or "tell you in a different way"? Do you model these strategies for children during your interactions?
4. What supports do you provide consistently to support following directions? Do you use gestures, pointing, repetition of directions, or breaking multistep directions into smaller units?
5. Are there children who would benefit from additional supports? What are those supports and how might you implement them? Remember to consider individual strengths when developing a plan for additional supports.

I am hopeful this chapter provided you with much deserved affirmation of the excellent ways you support the speech and language acquisition, development, and use in the natural early childhood education setting. I also hope that you have identified ways to continue to reflect on and enhance the natural early childhood education environment to provide supports to the diverse needs of the young learners in your classroom. Although each individual child has unique strengths and needs, these overarching strategies and tools can provide a supportive foundation for all young communicators to find success with engaging in play-based and early learning speech and language opportunities, including oral and written expression, as well as listening and reading comprehension. As we continue our conversation into Chapter 6, we will engage in discussion specific to young children who may demonstrate a need for a referral to a speech-language pathologist for a screening or assessment.

6

Children with Speech and Language Delays or Disorders

Children with speech and language delays and disorders experience the same need and want to effectively communicate with peers and adults that we all experience countless times daily, but they may experience more frequent unsuccessful, ineffective, or inefficient communication and interaction attempts. The function of successfully communicating provides a platform to get needs and wants met, decreases frustration and behaviors resulting from reduced or ineffective communication modes, allows individuals to follow directions, express feelings, and engage in reciprocal interactions. In considering the impact of ineffective and inefficient communication, we must consider the alternative results and impact of these interactions when a child experiences a communication breakdown. Educators and parents often ask, when is a referral for speech and language screening or assessment appropriate and necessary? Should I make the referral now or wait and see? Multiple variables are part of this discussion and determination, including exposure to language learning opportunities, chronological age, birth history, and cultural considerations. It is important to consider each child and family's individual situation and needs. The process of speech and language assessment is individualized based on a multitude of factors, including assurance that appropriate assessment tools are utilized, invitation for the family to actively engage in the process as a primary and central participant, and determining appropriate steps based on each child and family's individual strengths, needs, and desired outcomes.

Speech-language pathologists are identified as experts in the assessment and intervention of speech and language delays and disorders; however, it is essential to recognize that early childhood educators and parents are often the first people to identify a sound omission or substitution, note reduced speech clarity, suspect difficulty with rhyming, observe a limited vocabulary repertoire or use, difficulty asking or answering questions, or the inability to follow directions, to name a few areas of concern that may arise. This list is certainly not exhaustive in nature when considering speech and language difficulties; however, it begins to frame our discussion of when, why, and how to make a speech and language referral. As a speech-language pathologist, I often rely on collaborating team members, including education colleagues and parents, to work in partnership with me to identify when a child demonstrates areas of concern specific to speech and language within natural contexts, including the classroom, on the playground, in the cafeteria, in the home setting or in other environments of naturalistic early childhood engagement and interactions. Of course, the home environment is an important natural context during the early childhood years, making parents the most important and central team member during the referral and assessment process. In addition to parents and educators, physicians and other early childhood development partners may also be part of the speech and language screening and assessment referral process. There are multiple avenues for pursuit of a speech and language assessment, including early intervention, school-based, and clinical options. Families should be encouraged to determine the best avenue for referral and services based on their individual needs. Some families will choose to pursue multiple assessment and intervention options.

As we continue our discussion of assessment and intervention, it is important to keep in mind that the assessment process can feel overwhelming, confusing, and unclear to parents at times. Offering clear and concise information from the initial step of the process, combined with ongoing communication and opportunities to ask questions and offer information during the duration of the process, is the approach I always take and recommend when engaging with parents. I value parents as their child's primary caregiver, as well as the important role of a child's first teacher. My ongoing respect and value for parents continues to grow and I am fairly certain is infinitely impossible to measure because they are such an important and central part of the comprehensive assessment process. Parents know their child best, want what is best for their child, and strive to make the appropriate and necessary decisions to support their child with the information they have. This is the reason I see the parent as the most important and essential team member during the assessment process, as well as the planning and implementation of intervention. Does this mean the parent always has the answer to every question or that they always know the best next step at each point in the process? It doesn't because the process is one of gathering and obtaining relevant information, problem-solving, and adapting as a child and the family progress through the speech and language assessment and intervention process. Keep in mind that parents may experience fear, frustration, or stress linked to a child's speech or language deficits. Alternatively, parents will likely experience joy, excitement, and encouragement when a child progresses in developing and using new speech or language skills. In clinical practice, I have continued to engage in active listening and open communication with parents to build a working and collaborative partnership built upon trust. Working in partnership with the individuals consistently engaged in participating in a child's natural environment has the potential to support continued and optimal generalization of skills developed through intervention.

Screening and Assessment

The distinct difference between the purpose of a screening compared to a comprehensive assessment can be unclear to parents at times so ongoing communication is a key component of the assessment process. In many cases, I find that a family has a strong rapport with the child's teacher built upon ongoing communication and trust. These relationships are key to the child's success and the need for working together as a collaborative team. As a result, the teacher is another key team member during the assessment and intervention process. Teachers also know the child well and can offer valuable insight specific to communication within the natural context of the educational environment.

Let's begin our discussion with the different roles a screening and assessment play in the referral and evaluation process. In many cases, a screening may be the first step to identifying potential speech and language areas of concern. Screenings may be provided on a large scale, where, perhaps, an entire class is screened in some or all of the following areas: speech, language, voice, and fluency. Perhaps, you have experienced this universal screening at your early childhood site. One of our roles as speech-language pathologists is to identify young children who may not be meeting developmental milestones or following the typical developmental trajectories in the areas of speech and language. Universal screenings are a key way in which we can identify young children who may be at risk of speech and language delays or disorders, as well as identification of children who may benefit from a speech or language assessment to obtain additional information about the areas of concern. Alternatively, screening may be offered on an individual basis when a child is referred, due to specific speech or language concerns, in order to determine if additional information is needed to determine the presence of a speech or language delay or disorder. Comprehensive assessment, not screening, information will assist us in determining if there is a need for intervention. In both of these cases the purpose of screening doesn't change. Screenings are designed with the purpose of determining if additional information is needed and guide speech-language pathologists in determining what areas should be the focus of comprehensive assessment. Screenings don't provide diagnostic or prognostic information, but, instead, answer the following questions:

- Do we need to obtain additional information about speech or language areas of concern?
- In what speech or language areas do we need additional information?

When I administer a screening and the answer to the first question is "yes," I then ask myself the second question and gain my answers from the areas of the screening that indicated we need more information about the specified areas of speech and language. Screenings can be formal or informal in nature given that the purpose is to determine if additional information is needed to identify more comprehensive and specific information.

Now that we have identified the purpose of speech and language screenings, let's shift our discussion to comprehensive speech and language assessment. The comprehensive speech and language assessment process serves to provide important information about a child's strengths and areas of deficit. I want to ensure we recognize the importance and value of identifying the child's strengths during this process. Strengths can be utilized to support areas of difficulty. Identifying strengths early in the assessment process can offer valuable insight into effective ways to support the child through using these key skills, abilities, and traits. In addition, identification of a child's strengths can offer positive support to parents during a process that also identifies their child's areas of need. Parents may benefit from hearing both the individual positive strengths and areas in need of improvement to comprehensively understand their child's strengths and needs.

In addition to identifying strengths and areas of need, the speech and language assessment process guides the determination of diagnosis, need for services, prognosis, goal setting, and evidence-based intervention approach. Let's break down the reason that each of these components is valuable to the process. Diagnosis provides information about the nature of the deficit, including determination of speech and language delay, disorder, or difference. The determination of the need for appropriate and necessary services, based on areas of deficit, offers information related to the impact of the deficit on functional and effective communication. It is important to recognize that not every weakness or missing skill will require intervention. We must take into consideration several of the combined variables to determine the need for intervention, including developmental sequence, typical milestone markers, language and cultural considerations, and severity of the impact on effective functional communication. Prognosis offers insight into the course we can expect for progress. It may include the expected course of acquisition of the target skills and an expected timeframe for meeting the desired outcomes, as well as the overall expected progress. Finally, the comprehensive assessment process provides important information guiding the development of appropriate goal targets, service delivery model, and the recommended approach and frequency of intervention. The assessment process, when comprehensively implemented, identifies individual strengths and areas of speech and language deficit. The process allows us to discuss, develop, and implement a Plan of Care, Individual Family Service Plan (IFSP), or Individual Education Plan (IEP), depending on the clinical or educational practice setting and age of the child. The service and care plans include individualized and comprehensive targets to support the acquisition of developmentally appropriate skills or compensatory strategies to build bridges for strengthening effective and successful functional communication.

Delay, Disorder, Difference

One important component to consider within our assessment discussion is the important distinctions between a speech and language delay, disorder, and difference. Definition of these terms provides us information in order to assist with the understanding of important considerations during the assessment and intervention processes. It is important to consider each of these components and the accompanying definition. A speech or language delay indicates a child is following the typical trajectory of development meeting each milestone, but at a pace that is slower than typical developmental expectations. It is a delay in the development or use of speech or language, but typically progresses along the expected, developmental trajectory. Alternatively, a speech or language disorder indicates there are atypical characteristics of the progression of a child's communicative development along the expected trajectory of milestones. The child demonstrates a disorder in the ability to understand or produce the language code. In my clinical practice as a speech-language pathologist, regardless of the diagnosis of delay or disorder, my primary focus remains on determining the impact on effective functional communication. Determining the impact on functional communication serves to inform necessary goal setting in order to build an effective communication system within a child's natural environments, including home and school.

Finally, a speech or language difference indicates a child meets the speech and language norms of the primary language spoken, but may not meet the norms of the second language learned and spoken. In my personal clinical experience, this has occurred when a child enters a school where the primary spoken language is Standard American English (SAE), but the child speaks a language other than SAE. The child meets all speech and language development norms in the primary language but hasn't met the speech and language norms in Standard American English. It is important to note a speech or language difference is not a disorder or a delay and will not warrant speech or language intervention. In the case described above, we wouldn't expect children to meet the norms of Standard American English if they haven't been exposed to the second language expression or comprehension on a frequent and consistent basis as part of daily communication interactions. Grammatical errors, active listening without consistent expression, and switching between the primary and second languages are all typical and expected components of the second language acquisition process. Cummins

(1992) identified two stages of proficient second language acquisition, including basic interpersonal communication skills and cognitive academic language proficiency. Basic interpersonal communication can be described as social communication language and it may require between two to three years for a child to develop proficiency. Cognitive academic language proficiency includes formal academic language that is necessary for school success. Cognitive academic language may require between five to seven years to develop proficiency. This information provides insight into the reason some children learning a second language may flourish and grow at a faster rate with social communication on the playground or in the lunchroom but continue to experience communication challenges for a longer period within the formal classroom setting. It is important to note that, in these cases, assessment should account for these proficiency stages to ensure that a language difference is not misdiagnosed as a language delay or disorder.

Additionally, Roseberry-McKibbin (2018) outlined processes considered a typical part of the acquisition of a second language. The first process is identified as transfer indicating there is a transfer of first language communication behaviors to the second language. Fossilization, an identified process, indicates that even when a level of proficiency in the second language is reached, some second language errors persist. A second language-learner may also experience a silent period, a potentially three- to six-month time period of active listening with minimal speaking. Second language learners may also demonstrate interlanguage, indicating the development of an individualized linguistic system produced when attempting the second language. Language loss, indicating a decline in first language proficiency during second language learning, may also occur. Finally, code-switching may be common, with the second language learner alternating between the first and second language within a phrase, sentence, or conversation. The discussion of language differences and relevant considerations when determining the appropriate referral of a young child who is learning a second language are important. We need to consider these expected and normal processes that may occur as part of the second language learning process.

These considerations ensure appropriate diagnosis of language delays and disorders, as well as preventing misdiagnosis when there is a language difference.

Speech and Language Assessment Referral

I am going to provide general information specific to speech and language referrals, but I would encourage you to build a collaborative working relationship with the speech-language pathologist involved in your school or early childhood education program. Each young child is an individual and, as speech-language pathologists, we approach each situation with this important fact in mind. Consideration of developmental milestones, health history, the number of languages spoken, and cultural expectations and considerations need to be accounted for within the speech and language assessment and intervention processes. Although I can offer general insights into this process, based on my practical clinical experience and the evidence-based practice specific to speech and language assessment, your early childhood team, including the speech-language pathologist, should develop an appropriate system for determining the most appropriate processes and procedures for the speech and language screening and assessment process that is most effective in your setting. I would encourage you to engage in a conversation with the speech-language pathologist working with children in your classroom, at your school, in your early intervention program, or clinical setting to discuss specific referral information, including explanation of the process, when you should refer, and what information you may want to provide to the speech-language pathologist.

In my opinion, it is appropriate and important for a parent to refer a young child for a speech or language screening or assessment at any point during the early childhood years if they have any concerns about the child's form, content, or use of language. Parents may not state their concerns specific to form, content, or use, but generally will describe the actual speech or language concerns they are noticing. They may provide specific information with examples or they may identify that their child doesn't appear to be progressing in the areas of speech or language in comparison to other children the same age. It is my job as the speech-language pathologist, along with the parent and early childhood colleagues, to determine if a screening or comprehensive assessment is the recommended next step, as well as identify the specific areas to screen or assess. Chapter 2 provided a framework for developmental milestones to consider when determining if a young child is achieving speech and language milestones and following the sequence of development. If a child is not achieving speech and language developmental milestones or exhibits missing components of the typical speech and language developmental sequence, a referral for a speech and language screening or comprehensive assessment may be appropriate. Additionally, a young child who experiences frequent, ongoing communication breakdowns that negatively impact effective, functional communication may also benefit from a referral for speech and language assessment.

We need to consider the typical developmental norms and milestones when determining if a referral is appropriate. Let's take a moment to consider a child, who is three years old, exhibiting an incorrect production of the /r/ sound. Taking into consideration the age of the child, in conjunction with the developmental milestone expected for the accurate production and mastery of the /r/ as part of the later eight sounds, this would likely not warrant a referral for a speech sound assessment. However, we should account for how well the child is understood when speaking because reduced speech clarity, resulting from the production of /r/ may warrant consideration of a speech sound screening or assessment. Additionally, we need to consider details specific to the child's need linked to functional communication. For example, if the child's name begins with the /r/, we may, in fact, consider the appropriateness of working on the sound to support accurate production of the child's name. Alternatively, let's consider another example. If we consider a young child, who is 24 months old, with an expressive language inventory of two verbal words who is not utilizing other modes, such as gestures or pointing, to express, this would likely be an appropriate referral based on expectations for the typical language development trajectory of utilizing words, including two-word combinations to communicate by this child's age. Additionally, if the child is reported to be frustrated or is experiencing undesirable behaviors due to lack of communication, a referral would likely be an appropriate next step to consider. Using the information from Chapter 2, we can begin to identify when a speech and language referral for screening or assessment would be most appropriate; however, I want to encourage you to look comprehensively at each individual child's situation to determine if a referral would benefit a child and family. Continue to actively listen to concerns shared by a child's parents. Building open communication lines with the parent and speech-language pathologist can support a team approach in determining if and when referrals are necessary and appropriate.

Speech and Language Assessment Information

When a comprehensive speech and/or language assessment is determined to be the next most appropriate and necessary step, the process can be initiated. I want to emphasize the importance of the parent feeling comfortable and understanding the referral and the assessment. Prior to beginning the assessment process, I work to ensure the parent understands why an assessment is recommended, what will be assessed, and how the child will be assessed. I want teachers to understand all of these components also. Additionally, all members of the team will be invited to actively engage in the process. Utilizing a team approach will provide the most comprehensive understanding of the child's speech and language across various settings and with various communication partners. Do you see the link to generalization into the natural contexts? We can identify where the challenges are occurring in the natural environment and determine if the information aligns with standardized assessment measures, when appropriate, to help guide goal setting and ways to measure outcomes for optimal progress.

If you are currently an educator working in a classroom setting, you may already have a strong understanding of the speech and language assessment process, but I am going to provide some information about the process for the purpose of review or as an introduction for those who are less familiar with speech and language assessment. Speech-language pathologists will often administer formal, standardized speech and language assessments to determine current levels of performance. They may also complete observations, speech sound phonetic inventories, or language sampling within the natural context of the home or classroom environment. Recalling from earlier chapters, the goal of speech and language intervention is to support generalization of skills within the child's natural context. This requires us to understand the form, content, and use of language, as well as speech sound production and overall clarity within a child's natural contexts, including the classroom and home. Although formal, standardized assessments provide important information, it is imperative to determine the child's ability to communicate in natural contexts, within daily routines, and when participating in a variety of typical activities within the child's daily life. It is beneficial to look at consistencies and inconsistencies across various contexts, including formal testing and naturalistic situations. As we all are aware, young children may demonstrate differing communication behaviors or use of speech and language skills dependent upon the situation or environment. This is a key aspect I consider when completing an assessment. In some cases, parents or teachers report different skills or lack of skills than I am observing during completion of the assessment tasks. When this occurs, I find myself considering what additional information I need to obtain. Of course, parents and caregivers may, in fact, see different language use or speech production within daily contexts. Why does this occur? I often observe children and parents who have developed a communication system individualized to their life, their frequent and known contexts, and within their daily routines. It is often impressive to see the ease and fluency of these systems. Perhaps there are representational gestures or a specific word approximation recognized by the parent but not known to unfamiliar listeners. What does this tell me?

This is a significant strength that I always note within the context of my observations and reported information. The child has demonstrated the ability to develop a systematic and effective communication mode to functionally communicate. Although this isn't the ultimate goal because we want children to be able to communicate across various contexts with familiar and unfamiliar listeners, it points to problem-solving and motivation to communicate. Additionally, a teacher may report similar information, including a systematic way a child communicates with peers within the classroom effectively even when speech or language deficits are apparent. The alternate can also be true. Based on assessment information, I may find a young child has solid skills in the areas of vocabulary or following directions, but the child is unable to utilize these skills within the natural environment. Remember, this is an issue with the use of language and the generalization of functional communication in various areas of the child's life, both school and home. A comprehensive speech and language assessment will gather information from parent(s) and teachers, and include observations within natural environments, administration, analysis, and interpretation of standardized assessments. A comprehensive assessment will provide us specific, analyzed, and synthesized information to determine if speech and language deficits are present, if the deficits require intervention, guidance for goal development, and prognostic markers.

Talking with Parent(s)

Children interact across various situations and with many people in their lives who love and care for them. I am using the term parent in this book, but I recognize that children may have guardians, other than parents, or an alternative living and custody situation. Regardless of these varied and individualized situations, I maintain my focus on working collaboratively with the family unit to support the child and family. I am often asked by educators: "How do you approach the speech or language concern with the parent?" That is a valid question and educators often want to ensure they only begin this discussion when it is appropriate. I believe honest and factual discussion with a solid base in care for the child is a strong approach. Parents vary in their knowledge of typical speech and language development. Parents may also respond in a variety of different ways when approached with concerns about a child's speech and/or language functioning. It is my role and responsibility as a speech-language pathologist to support them in understanding the various components, domains, and modalities of speech and language acquisition, development, and use specific to their individual child when a potential delay or disorder may be present. The reason I bring this topic to our discussion is because I find active listening beneficial. What is the parent telling us? The parent likely knows the child better than all of us. I mentioned in an earlier chapter that I view parents as the most important member of the child's team. We are afforded the opportunity to walk alongside the parent and offer support to the child and family. Engaging parents from the beginning and ensuring they understand their value to the team, builds a positive rapport with the potential for a continued collaborative focus. What does this offer us in regards to prognosis? Parents and caregivers interact with children in natural settings, right? The overall goal is functional and effective communication in natural environments. Parents and caregivers are the members of the team who can provide us information and access to supporting another natural context and the ability to promote generalization.

We now return to our discussion of how do we talk to parents when we have a concern. Working collaboratively with the speech-language pathologist connected to your program or classroom, combined with references to typical speech and language development information, offer a strong foundation for identifying the appropriate discussion of speech and language screening and assessment referrals. Building trust and partnerships with families, from the beginning, is always best practice and helpful when we need to discuss potential referrals. It is another reason I value my work with early childhood educators because parent engagement is a hallmark pillar of early childhood programming. Beginning conversations discussing a young child's strengths is a great place to start. Each and every child has undeniable individual strengths that make him or her unique. Sharing those strengths and actively listening to parents share additional strengths is generally where I begin. I approach my parent interactions in this way regardless of whether the parent appears to have awareness of concerns or not. It is always important to identify a young child's strengths because, as you recall from previous discussion, they are an important part of speech and language assessment and intervention considerations. As you begin to navigate the discussion of areas of concern, it can be helpful to outline observations you have made or specific speech or language situations that have occurred in the classroom setting. Be specific and provide details. Parents want to understand the what, how, and why if possible. In some cases, the details allow them to connect to similar situations they have observed. If you begin your conversation with a parent stating that a child doesn't categorize or answer questions, this doesn't provide specific or concrete information. Instead, consider stating that the child answers accurately when asked his name and age, but during circle time or art isn't able to accurately answer questions such as, "What do you use to eat soup" when reading a story about a boy eating soup or "What do we do with scissors" when participating in a cutting activity. Perhaps, you may explain that a young child is able to follow routine single step directions; however, more complex multistep directions, including descriptive words, result in a decreased ability to complete the requested direction. These conversations are an excellent time to listen to the information a parent is willing and able to share. We can learn more about the child's speech and language skills in other contexts through the shared information. Perhaps, a child is quiet and uses minimal verbal communication at school, but talks frequently at home. This is valuable information to help us understand a child's communication profile.

After the initial discussion or in some cases, multiple conversations, if a parent agrees to a recommended speech and language screening or assessment, it is helpful to ensure that the child's parent understands the process and once again, feels like a partner from the beginning. This is another point in the process where a collaborative and ongoing working relationship with the speech-language pathologist is valuable. Your ongoing collaboration will afford you the opportunity to explain the process to the parent or connect the parent to the speech-language pathologist to ask questions and gain additional information.

Assessments often involve paperwork, including social and developmental histories, permissions, and other information gathering tools. Please keep in mind, this can be overwhelming. The goal is to open up lines of communication from the beginning of the process. In cases where the child is in a school environment, the teacher may have already established a positive working relationship with the family so I will often engage the teacher to help me ensure the family feels supported and comfortable asking questions. Please don't assume if a family doesn't follow through with paperwork or the assessment process that they aren't interested or that they don't want support for their child. Life is complex with multiple facets. If we do our best to listen and understand parents' hopes, concerns, and questions related to their child, we can walk together while working as a team. We can create collaborative opportunities built on trust and partnership. At times, the process moves slower than we would like. Other times, the process is slower than parents prefer. Open communication goes a long way in helping us navigate a sometimes overwhelming process and potentially difficult conversations. Ensure the family feels the collaborative approach working with them, rather than a process happening to them. As a speech-language pathologist, I want to be part of the team, along with parents and educators. Building a strong working relationship with your speech-language pathologist is a great place to start! If you don't know the speech-language pathologist at your school or you haven't found an opportunity to meet yet, take time to introduce yourself and begin a discussion about referral, assessment, and intervention processes and procedures.

I recognize and understand that discussions related to areas of speech and language concerns can be difficult to initiate. The important focus is the ongoing conversation and open lines of communication with all members of the team to the extent possible. As we work towards effective functional communication for young communicators with speech and language deficits, we need to maintain awareness of our ongoing and collaborative communication with parents. As we transition to the final chapter of this book, we will visit final thoughts about communication breakdowns and additional considerations that are important to continuing the discussion of supporting young communicators in acquiring, developing, and using effective speech and language during the early childhood years, building a foundation for future language and literacy learning.

Bibliography

Cummins, J. (1992). Language proficiency, bilingualism, and academic achievement. In P. A. Richard-Amato & M. A. Snow (Eds.), *The Multicultural Classroom: Readings for Content-area Teachers* (pp. 16–27). New York, NY: Longman.

Roseberry-McKibbin, C. (2018). *Multicultural Students with Special Language Needs* (5th ed.). Ocean-side, CA: Academic Communication Associates.

7

The Communication Breakdown

The previous chapters of this book have explored various components of language, speech, and literacy, including developmental expectations and trajectories. We have discussed the form, content, and use of language, as well as speech sound production and the relationship to speech intelligibility. We have explored theoretical constructs and associated classic theorists, providing insight into research specific to the acquisition, development, and use of language modalities. Consideration of the classroom setting and ways to support children in navigating and learning language through play-based interactions has been a focus to promote generalization of language skills across natural contexts. The impact of these language domains and modalities on effective and functional communication has become evident as we have explored the multiple variables of the functional communication system. It is important, as we summarize our discussion, to revisit the importance and need for all individuals to access and experience effective use of communication in order to engage in a variety of meaningful interactions and communication exchanges across natural environments. As we have discussed, it isn't enough for children to learn and master speech and language skills in a single environment or for a specific scenario. We should strive to support children through planting communication seeds for continued speech and language development, as well as build bridges when needed to ensure optimal communication experiences.

Communication is a social experience that comprises the combination of verbal and non-verbal systems of communicative behaviors, providing opportunities for engaging in functional, effective, and meaningful interactions with peers and adults, across a variety of daily contexts, activities, and routines. Communication provides a means to communicate for various functions, including requesting, commenting, and sharing ideas. As we have explored and gained a greater understanding of the complexity of communication exchanges, it is important to identify, consider, revisit, and review the various factors that may result in disruption of the effective and functional communication process. These disruptions and barriers impacting effective and functional communication exchanges can occur due to a variety of challenges, many outlined in the previous chapters.

As you reflect on the information you have read and considered, you may have new ideas or understanding of communication breakdowns with young communicators that you have observed or experienced, in your classroom. Perhaps, a young child didn't have the vocabulary or background knowledge to express his or her wants and needs. A young child may not have demonstrated the vocabulary knowledge to express emotions, resulting in acting out or shutting down behaviors. Perhaps you are revisiting or gaining the understanding that behavior is communication. There is a message within the context of a child's behavior, including the verbal and nonverbal communication. Hopefully, you are now able to consider that these behaviors may, in fact, be based in growing and ongoing frustration. Is it possible the child in your class who doesn't consistently follow directions or offers related, but inaccurate, answers to questions you ask, may have underlying speech and language difficulties, resulting from gaps in expressive or receptive language acquisition, development, or use? Is it possible these gaps impact his or her ability to effectively participate in the various communication exchanges within the natural environment? Have you considered the young child who quietly plays alone but doesn't exhibit any challenging behaviors? Given the information we have explored in the previous chapters, would you consider asking the question, does the young child have the communication skills of initiation and maintenance of sustained communication exchanges to engage with same-aged peers? Perhaps you are more attuned to the nonverbal communication of a young child who has reduced speech clarity when communicating, but who is able to utilize pointing and gestures to express within your classroom environment. In practice, these are all examples of scenarios I have encountered with young children. It is possible you have also observed or experienced similar scenarios within various contexts when interacting with young children. Have you considered it is possible these exhibited behaviors, reactions, or responses may be masking an underlying communication deficit? If you have considered this possibility, I hope you will continue to engage in the reflective practice, problem-solving, and critical thinking linked to ensuring an optimal communication environment for all young communicators in your life. If you are finding yourself exploring new considerations, I hope you will find encouragement in this book's discussion to investigate the complexities of speech, language, and literacy.

When we take into consideration that a child's frustration, due to a lack of effective communication exchanges, may potentially result in shutting down and retreating from social interactions, it seems reasonable to pause and explore the reasons for a child's behaviors. In many situations, we just need to shift, modify, and adapt the lens we are looking through to see the underlying cause of behaviors, responses, reactions, and interactions. A slight shift of the lens we look through, in order to analyze a specific situation, can offer insight that can change the trajectory of a child's communication attempts in a positive way, through planting seeds, breaking down barriers, and building bridges to support the development of stronger speech, language, and literacy foundational skills.

Given that we communicate with a variety of familiar and unfamiliar communication partners in a variety of known and unknown contexts, it is inevitable that communication breakdowns will occur for all of us at some point. Communication breakdowns are a natural part of the communication process. We have all experienced breakdowns in our communication at some point. Perhaps, we have learned from these communication breakdowns. It is possible in these situations that we have learned ways to navigate, clarify, or offer additional information to guide the communication interaction towards a successful encounter. If we abandoned the attempt, did we take the opportunity to reflect about the potential barriers and future solutions. If we persisted, what strategies or tools worked to successfully communicate. In much the same way we analyze our own communication attempts and interactions, we can begin to identify, critically think, and problem-solve ways to support our young communicators when communication breakdowns occur in their interactions. As they are learning language, they may need support with navigation to clarify, restate, or provide additional information in order to increase the effectiveness of the communication encounter.

Even the most skilled and effective communicators experience breakdowns at times. It is not a surprise that young children learning the form, content, and use of language experience communication breakdowns. In addition, when we consider our young communicators with speech and language delays or disorders, we would expect communication breakdowns to find their way into their communication attempts and interactions. Reflecting on the cause of the breakdown, determining appropriate strategies to navigate these situations, and exploring ways to build strong future communication, builds communicative effectiveness. The ability to achieve a level of communicative effectiveness is motivating for continued practice and exploration with the use of language in order to communicate messages successfully. We need to maintain awareness and acceptance that communication breakdowns, including the inability to effectively express or understand, are also a typical part of acquiring and developing communication skills during the early childhood years. We strive to build background knowledge and increase a child's vocabulary inventory, practice asking and answering questions, and expand direction following skills through experiences and opportunities for young children to learn and practice language, through play-based, social, and literacy interactions.

Young children learn to interact within daily interactions and communicate effectively with a variety of communication partners through the various interactions and opportunities for practice offered in your classrooms and homes on a daily basis. Speech, language, and literacy can be learned through intentional play-based opportunities and teachable moments, opening important doors to increased vocabulary learning and language use opportunities. Consider the young child who learns to express frustration using words or pointing to a picture through practice over a variety of scenarios, including interactive book reading introducing and highlighting emotion words, large group discussion about vocabulary specific to emotions, and opportunities to process through an emotional experience with a caring adult. Perhaps, the young child knocked over a block tower in frustration prior to learning and practicing alternative ways to express frustration, related to difficulty with the task of stacking the blocks. Now, the young child has the opportunity to respond in a new way built upon the foundation of new knowledge, vocabulary, language models, and opportunities for practice, in order to support an appropriate language and behavior response to frustration. Keep in mind, having moments of frustration in life are expected and we have the opportunity to build the vocabulary and appropriate responses to these life situations in the early childhood classroom, along with, providing opportunities to practice in a safe and secure environment with caring and supportive adults, using play-based interactions. This is a single example of the way we are able to provide language learning opportunities through play and daily interaction to build a stronger and more robust language system. Generalization of this concept to a variety of vocabulary building, language formulation and grammatical structure, and language use opportunities is embedded within early childhood education classrooms and homes each and every day. The opportunities for learning and practice are endless within the daily activities, routines, and interactions. Parents and teachers are building more communication bridges for children each day than they ever will realize, simply through building background knowledge, identifying contextual cues, modeling effective communication, and providing a safe and supportive place to learn and practice developing communication skills. I have personally observed so many of these opportunities firsthand. I have the opportunity to see the value of these learning processes unfold and grow into successful future speech, language, and literacy foundational pieces positively impacting learning and effective functional communication.

As you continue to reflect and consider ways you are able to continue incorporating current and new ways of building communication bridges for young children, in order to support the effective communication that all individuals desire each day, I would encourage you to consider each communication breakdown as an opportunity to identify the strengths, determine the barriers, analyze the communication behaviors, and problem-solve ways to support effective communication. Simply refocusing the lens that we look through when these communication breakdowns occur can offer new insight into the cause and potential solutions for future communication effectiveness. In my role as a speech-language pathologist, I am often asked, what do you or what should we work on first? My answer is always the same and is a relatively simple answer. It is likely the answer you would expect after reading the information in the previous chapters. I continue to emphasize the essential need to support effective and functional communication for all young communicators, providing them a solid and strong platform to share ideas, convey thoughts, respond to language input, and engage in meaningful interactions. In my clinical practice, I always strive to determine the ways that I can focus on improving the specific communication skills or the use of those skills, in order to provide the greatest positive impact on overall effective and functional communication. My goal is to increase the positive communication exchanges for a young communicator, in order to strengthen communication confidence and effectiveness. Based on our ongoing discussion in this book, we know, without any doubt, communication is a complex, dynamic, and at times challenging process. Maintaining a focus on the generalization of effective communication will continue to guide us towards meaningful discussion to identify and analyze barriers and then allow us to shift our focus to solution-based problem-solving.

As we bring our discussion to a close, I hope you have found some concrete strategies for supporting speech and language acquisition, development, and use that you can easily implement with all children in your classroom or young children in your home to support effective functional communication exchanges. I am also hopeful that you have found affirmation and admiration for the wonderfully meaningful work you engage in each day. The ongoing commitment of parents, early childhood educators, and early elementary educators to build a strong speech and language foundation for future language and literacy learning and growth is a valuable asset to each young child's current communication and has individual optimal future potential when built upon a solid foundation. Having a mode of communication empowers young children to share their ideas, understand the world around them, and engage in meaningful exchanges with peers and adults. This is what I want for each of the children I have the opportunity to support. I know you likely share a similar hope for each of the young children in your lives. Finally, I want to bring us back to a central and key final thought. I continue to learn so much about what a young child needs for communication through observation and interaction with the young child and the family. We need to continue to focus on individual child and family needs to ensure that the communication bridges built to support effective communication are appropriate based on the needs specific to each child and family. As you continue to process the information in this book, you may find it beneficial to explore additional research and evidence-based practice, and reflect with a deeper consideration of the specific details related to communication breakdowns, while ensuring the important facet of each child as an individual with unique strengths and needs is preserved in each individual case of speech, language, and literacy learning. Take time to actively listen and engage with the family, while also learning from the child.

Young children teach us a great deal about persistence, resilience, and motivation. Let's follow their lead and keep learning and growing through play-based and literacy-learning activities, along with them. I find it appropriate to end this final chapter with a reminder from Chapter 1. I want to encourage us to continue the important teamwork to advocate for our young communicators and provide a robust, language-rich environment full of opportunities for speech and language practice, supportive bridges when necessary, and the ongoing planting of speech and language learning seeds, nurtured as the young child experiences the joy of successful communication interactions. Because, please remember my early childhood friends and colleagues, *Communication always counts*!

Printed in the United States
By Bookmasters